A TRAILS BOOKS GUIDE

GREAT MINNESOTA TAVERNS

DAVID K. WRIGHT & MONICA G. WRIGHT

TRAILS BOOKS
Black Earth, Wisconsin

Library of Congress Catalog Card Number: 2002105661
ISBN: 1-931599-12-2

Copy Editor: Jerry Minnich
Designer: Jennifer Walde
Cover Designer: Jennifer Walde

Front Cover: The interior of the tavern known as Pracna on Main Street, the
historic dining saloon overlooking the Mississippi River and downtown Minneapolis.

Printed in the United States of America by McNaughton & Gunn.

06 05 04 03 02   6 5 4 3 2 1

Trails Books, a division of Trails Media Group, Inc.
P.O. Box 317 • Black Earth, WI 53515
(800) 236-8088 • e-mail: books@wistrails.com
www.trailsbooks.com

To Tucker Minash,
who usually knew when to say when.

MINNESOTA

CONTENTS

CENTRAL MINNESOTA

SOUTHERN MINNESOTA

MINNEAPOLIS AND VICINITY

ST. PAUL AND VICINITY

HASTINGS

LAKELAND

NORTH ST. PAUL

STILLWATER

APPENDIX A

APPENDIX B

PREFACE

There were two sources for a cold beer in a little Indiana town near where the elder of us grew up. One catered to retired men and closed every day at 6 p.m. The other served bikers. It was the only beer joint known where the bars affixed to the windows were on the inside. Unless padlocked by the authorities, the place was always open.

How times change. Today, every municipality of any size has at least one safe, clean, comfortable, and atmospheric tavern where folks are greeted with a smile and where the beverages are a cut above the average supermarket twelve-pack. This book is our effort to track down such emporia in Minnesota.

We know, we know, several thoughts come immediately to mind. First, some readers will deem it a snap to find dozens of great beer places in the Twin Cities alone. While that is possible, we invite you to consider destinations both urban and rural—Minnesota has an encouraging number of bars, taverns, brewpubs, etc., all across the state. Second, a few readers will search in vain in this book for their favorite watering hole and fail to find it. To you we say, let us know about it for the next edition. Third, others will realize that this modest volume is a dandy excuse to check out places we might otherwise drive by. Guilty as charged.

To orient the prospective beer drinker, we have included both straightforward and whimsical details about areas where the bars are located; listings for finding bar, brewpub, or microbrewery Web sites; for dining in places where the food is exceptional; and for taking the opportunity to visit nearby attractions. Information on matters such as hours is also included.

Finally, an admonishment and an assist. Places serving the public may occasionally be hard to find, or they may change hands or names almost overnight. To help counter that possibility, we've included directions, where necessary. That is so you can find the front door on your way in. Finding the front door on your way out is your responsibility.

Prosit,

David K. Wright, Monica G. Wright

Summer 2002

INTRODUCTION
Minnesota

Hurray for Minnesota, the home or birthplace of artificial turf, Betty Crocker, Bob Dylan, Charlie Brown, Cheerios, Cream of Wheat, Dairy Queen, Garrison Keillor, The Great Gatsby, Greyhound buses, Jessie Ventura, Jessica Lang, the Jolly Green Giant, Judy Garland, Lucky Lindy, Main Street, "The Mary Tyler Moore Show," Malt-o-Meal, Paul Bunyan, Pearson Nut Rolls, the Pillsbury Dough Boy, Scotch Tape, sandpaper, Spam, snowmobiles, Wheaties, Winona Ryder, and other people and things too numerous to mention. It is also as good a state as any for visiting taverns.

For the sake of convenience, Minnesota is divided into five areas in this beer-hunting book. They are Northern Minnesota, Central Minnesota, Southern Minnesota, Minneapolis and vicinity, and St. Paul and vicinity. This was done for the sake of convenience and based very roughly on how and where people travel, plus the distribution of population. There are other factors to be considered, such as which ethnic groups drink the most beer. We did not attempt to answer that question, but instead left it for tavern customers to ponder.

Perhaps the best way to understand this vast, thinly populated place would have been to divide it according to vegetation. Pick up any state tourism booklet and you will learn that there are three major types of countryside in Minnesota. Nearly half of the state is pinelands—there are 38 million acres of conifers. That half runs approximately from just north of St. Cloud to the Canadian border, and from west of Lake Itasca to Lake Superior. Hardwoods are found in a northwest-to-southeast swath that widens as it heads south, making up about one-quarter of the terrain. Prairies, configured in somewhat the same shape, also widen in the south and cover one-quarter of the map.

Why does all this matter? Primarily, it offers visitors nice counterpoints from one region to another. It also tells us something about the amounts of precipitation (more needed by the pines, less needed by prairie wildflowers) in various locales. As for the thousands of lakes, most can be found in the piney woods. This is an accident of ancient glacial movement, though, rather than one of precipitation. All in all, one could hardly ask for more variety in a relatively flat, northern climate.

One other quirk of nature should be noted. The Red River, which has been chosen to form much of the western border, is one of the very few rivers in the United States to flow north. While it has laid down one of the most fertile valleys on earth, this northerly flow causes great woe among riverbank residents. Since ice melts first in the south, the Red turns to liquid and flows north, often overrunning its own icy body and causing devastating floods. Flooding has been so nasty in the last few years that East Grand Forks, Minnesota, gave serious thought to changing its name. As if that might help.

What does all this have to do with drinking a cold beer in a friendly tavern? (Please work with us here.) Water—the cleaner the better—is responsible both for the well-being of Minnesotans and the quality of a bracing brew. It is everywhere here, forming a lovely, lakey, backdrop to a modest small town, moving grain and coal up and down the Mississippi, or replenishing a favorite up-north fishing hole. The Great Canadian Shield, an ancient piece of rock that covers part of the state just a few feet beneath the soil, also shields the water many folks here enjoy drinking. The pristine liquid is part of what makes the local beer so clean and tasty.

Or is it the tangy air? The weather here is bracing, to say the least, with as much temperature variation as any state in the lower 48. In July, for example, the prairie can be poaching in 100-plus degree heat, while the North Shore experiences a lake breeze that keeps the thermometer at around 50. There is not a lot of snow in Minnesota, but with the aid of a stiff wind it can drift as high as a small silo or a big truck. Give the residents credit—they hardly ever let the climate keep them from going out.

Therefore, expect to get a decent representation of Minnesotans in virtually any tavern in this book. Lean on them for advice on accommodations, on the best beers to sample, the best routes to take, and those activities that most tourists will miss. The world's biggest ball of string? Take this route. That Minneapolis museum devoted to medical oddities? Go here. The best seats in the Metrodome? Request this section.

Newer than anywhere east, greener than anywhere west, tidier than anywhere south, warmer than the Arctic Circle, Minnesota and its taverns are sites to behold and enjoy.

ACKNOWLEDGMENTS

Many, many thanks to the rank-and-file tavern employees in Minnesota. There really is something to being "Minnesota nice," and they proved it with their collective patience.

NORTHERN
Minnesota

W HEN Americans think of Minnesota, their mental pictures almost invariably are of the north. Towering pines, crystal lakes, thundering falls, meadows with hardy grasses and short, stubborn wildflowers, towns that get along just fine without cable television, long winter nights alight with stars, leaping fish and skittish moose, individuals as rugged as their surroundings. There may be other aspects to Minnesota, but none so traditionally and vividly etched.

And why not? Generations of people from all over the Midwest can recall long summer vacation days on one of the thousands of lakes up this way. The mosquito bites and the surprise thunderstorms fade from memory, while the sheer beauty and the crackle of a campfire linger forever in a visitor's mind. There are, however, four seasons here; fall and winter seem to arrive way too early, while spring and summer show up only with reluctance.

There is a real spirit of enterprise here. Nicely maintained, if remote, resorts dot the coniferous northeast, while towns that may have started with the construction of a sawmill can be found in midstate, in the thin band of hardwoods running southeast from Canada. The northern prairie pushes well into Manitoba and is peopled by folks who have done everything from invent the snowmobile to populate the National Hockey League.

This is a place where pregnant women sometimes move into the nearest town, several miles away, to ensure that they can reach the hospital at the proper time. It is a part of the United States where a visitor can drive for several miles along a national highway without spotting another vehicle. And it is where sometimes-endangered wildlife such as wolves, moose, and eagles are common sights. Northern Minnesota is not for the squeamish or the fastidious, but the vast majority of tavern patrons and other residents would have it no other way.

BEMIDJI

Bemidji looks so remote on the state map, travelers might assume it is in either North Dakota or Manitoba. As it turns out, the small city is a true northern oasis, with nice residences and a state university, nestled with Lake Bemidji, Lake Irving, and the Mississippi River. Neither large (12,200 residents at last count) nor pretentious, Bemidji will strike visitors as self-sufficient, having a busy downtown, an imposing statue of Paul Bunyan and Babe the Blue Ox, and dozens of resorts and lodges on the many nearby lakes. Best of all, this is the first municipality downriver from the source of the Mississippi. How many towns can make that claim?

(For more information, telephone (800) 458-2223, or contact these Web sites: www/visitbemidji.com, www.bemidji.org, or www.minnesotanorthwoods.com.)

First City Brewery & Grill

128 First Street West (Union Square)
Bemidji, MN 56601
Telephone: (218) 751-9261
Hours: 11 a.m.-1 a.m. (bar); 11 a.m.-10 p.m. Sunday-Thursday, 11 a.m.-11 p.m. Friday-Saturday (kitchen); closed major holidays.
Nearby attraction: Lake Itasca, source of the Mississippi River, is southwest of town.

Chances of catching a passenger train from Union Station are slim, but the odds of obtaining a craft beer from the brewery inside this popular restaurant are excellent.

The station, which was built in 1911, was rehabbed into a restaurant in 1976. The brewpub was created in 1997 and is billed as the only such place in a big triangle between Duluth and Fargo. First City offers half a dozen distinctive, fresh brews, most of which carry the railroad theme. They include:
- **Golden Spike Ale**, a light but malty brew, made with two kinds of West Coast hops and with barley malt from Munich.

First City Brewery & Grill, Bemidji.

- **First Street Wheat** leaves a crisp aftertaste, with just a hint of honey. Like all of the brewpub's products, there is a light but discernible hopped flavor.

- **Seasonal Express Ales** are brewed in small (eight-keg) batches and tend to be heftier in winter and lighter in summer.

- **Coal Train Porter** is a nice play on words (the railroad, Cole Porter?) and is the darkest brew on tap. Five malts are used to drop hints of espresso and caramel.

- **Cannon Ball Red Ale** displays a copper-red color and a rich bouquet of floral hops.

- **Orient Express India Pale Ale** offers a strong and aggressive presence of hops, imported from England.

Purists can purchase a sample of the brews in a little six-pack of glasses. For the not-so-purist, there is a tapper for Michelob Golden Light, plus well-stocked wine and liquor service.

This is a large place, with three dining rooms and separate menus for the bar and the restaurant. The bar has a nice variety of appetizers, soups, salads, burgers and other sandwiches, pastas, and pizzas. Signature items on the bar menu include a spicy chicken or a beef sirloin fajita. Food that looks especially promising to the committed beer drinker includes appetizers such as smoked, scotch-marinated salmon, served with capers, onions, tartar sauce and French bread, or mushroom burgundy sauté. Pizzas come in personal or couples sizes and feature standard toppings as well as such creative fare as pesto, Alfredo sauce, or chicken.

The menu states that Union Station is the "Grand Steakhouse of the Northwoods," though in truth the kitchen serves a wide range of food. Steaks are cooked on a grill fired with hickory, the most popular cut being a petite New York sirloin. In contrast, the vegetarian platter is furnished with wild rice bread and an assortment of sautéed mushrooms and other veggies. Look, too, for appetizers, main-dish salads, ribs, pastas, other steaks and chops, combinations, and desserts.

Returning to the bar, which is solid and in keeping with such a historic building, a visitor will find a nice cross-section of northerners. The kids with their baseball caps worn backwards are college students, while the older men and women work locally. A fellow at the bar, who travels, said over a glass of porter that he stays overnight in Bemidji whenever possible, so he can avail himself of the beer and ale varieties here. He also noted that the restaurant serves all the crab legs one cares to eat every Sunday. And there is alfresco dining in warm weather. All solid reasons for paying a call.

DETROIT LAKES

A with-it town of 7,405 some 45 miles east of Fargo, Detroit Lakes is surrounded by hundreds of bodies of water and dozens of fishing and related resorts. This is the nearest municipality of any size to Tamarac National Wildlife Refuge, a 43,000-acre tract with 200 bird species, including the bald eagle. The town offers all of the usual winter sports, and there is Detroit Mountain for downhill skiing—a rarity anywhere near the prairie. Glaciers created the lakes here, including the big twin lake on the south side that is the local namesake.

(For more information, call (800) 542-3992 or check this Web site: www.visitdetroitlakes.com. For fishing or for snow conditions, dial (800) 433-1888.)

Lakeside Bar and Grill

200 West Lake Drive
Detroit Lakes, MN 56501
Telephone: (218) 847-7887
Hours: 11 a.m.-midnight (bar); 11 a.m.-10 p.m. (kitchen).
Closed Thanksgiving and Christmas.
Nearby attraction: Detroit Lake is across the street.

Chet, the manager of Lakeside, and Rick, the owner of the tavern critiqued next, are good friends. Their establishments face sprawling Detroit Lake and are only a block apart. In the summer, the places overflow with *turistas*, those relentless vacationers who come from Iowa or southern Minnesota or who-knows-where for a week or more to fish, swim, drink, and dine. Things calm a bit in the winter, as the locals regain control and the ice fishers and snowmobilers recreate. Though we did not see it, perhaps there is a well-worn path between their two spots and the body of water.

In all likelihood, Lakeside was here first. The current owners report that it was opened in 1891 as a hotel. The bar and grill still operate out of the venerable building, but it has been years since guests stayed over. These days, the hungry and the thirsty consume on a spacious deck at umbrella tables, enjoying what has to be 18 hours of sunlight in late June. This is as good a place as any, weather permitting, for watching the world go by over the rim of a beer glass.

That reminds us . . . There are several intriguing taps here, not the least of which is Anchor Steam, the stalwart brew from San Francisco. There are other micro and mini brews, plus Killian's Red, Budweiser Light, and Miller Lite. Numerous beers may be had by the bottle, and there is a nice selection of wine and liquor. Cable TV's trusty service delivers a variety of music; you can tell what kind of mood the help is in by the choice and volume of the tunes!

Patrons do not live on beer alone—at least they had better not try. Instead, check out what's for lunch. The most popular sandwich is the Chicken Impressionist, a chunk of breast meat with a slice of Swiss cheese and trimmings. In the evening, a New York strip steak heads a complete menu. This is more conventional food than the Italian-Mexican offerings at Zorbaz, although each is a nice counterpoint to the other.

Zorbaz

408 West Lake Drive
Detroit Lakes, MN 56501
Telephone: (218) 847-5305
Web site: http://detroitlakes.com/zorbaz/
Hours: 11 a.m.-1 a.m. Closed Christmas Eve.
Nearby attraction: Detroit Lake is across the street.

One of seven Zorbaz restaurants in Minnesota (the eighth is in Fargo), this place is a beer drinker's heaven. Gleaming in a formidable row behind the bar are 30 beer taps. Out of sight (but not out of mind) are 70 different beers in bottles. The tap handles are fun reading: Berger, Boddington Pub Ale, Breckinridge Avalanche, Breckinridge India Pale Ale, La Trappe Ale, Pacifico, at least three kinds of Schell, Sierra Nevada Pale Ale, Three Floyds, etc. The stalks showing Budweiser and Bud Light get lost amid their exotic brethren.

It's fun to sit near the draft handles and see what folks are consuming. This is a neighborhood tavern across the street from a big lake, and fathers and mothers may be enjoying bottles of Newcastle Ale while their kids, up here for the weekend from Minneapolis, are dealing with a pitcher of Schell Schmalt'z Alt. The more adventurous may order a shot of any of 50 different brands of tequila (depending on availability), or some other liquor.

But beer is the popular drink at Zorbaz, perhaps because it goes so well with the food. The menu is a real surprise up this way: It dares to offer either Italian or Mexican fare and goes even farther by occasionally mixing the cuisines. The Mexican pizza is popular to the point that it has been the subject of a national magazine article. The primary dining difference between summer and winter is that more pasta is served in winter months.

Zorbaz, Detroit Lakes.

Rick, who owns this Zorbaz, notes that nachos and mini-pizzas are high-demand luncheon items, while pizza and Mexican dinners head out of the kitchen for dinner. "You wouldn't expect it, this far north, but our beans and sauces are fresh," he says.

Zorbaz is an easy place to fill in the summer, what with the beach and places like a souvenir T-shirt shop nearby. There is patio dining, plus toys such as a pool table, a foosball table, and a dartboard outside under a tent. In the winter, locals populate the restaurant, secure in the knowledge that the tourists are some distance away. Speaking of distance, the tavern is about a mile south of the main part of town. Head south on Washington Avenue, then turn west on West Lake Drive.

Winter or summer visitor, the facility peddles T-shirts, sweatshirts, caps, some specialty clothing—and Zorbaz's own hot sauce. Those who wonder how the locals stay warm year round can sample the hot sauce and understand. Any time of the year, this informal place with the black-and-white checkered floor tile is a nice refuge from sun or snow.

DULUTH

Do folks in Duluth know how to party? A while back, a couple of local fire-fighters were disciplined after one of two civilian women broke their ankles sliding too swiftly down the fire pole. Seems the girls were at a bar when a bachelor party broke out, they were invited back to the station, and one thing led to another. Accidents, happily, are few and far between at most taverns and attractions.

The city's big attraction, of course, is Lake Superior. Containing as much water as the other four Great Lakes combined, or about ten percent of the fresh surface water *on earth*, Lake Superior forms the east side of town and sets the stage for everything from a stunning sunrise to an invigorating swim. To anyone not used to living on or very near big water, the vast, cold body looks at best sullen. How must it have appeared to Daniel Greysolon sieur Du Luth, who arrived with a canoeing party in 1679, half a century after the first voyageurs visited this immense natural harbor?

Even earlier, Sioux lived along the shores. They were replaced by Ojibwa (Chippewa), who moved in from the east, trying to stay ahead of white settlers. Later on, in 1855, a canal was opened at Sault Sainte Marie, Michigan, that allowed boats to sail between Lake Superior and the lower Great Lakes. Timber and iron ore in mind-boggling quantities moved through the twin ports of Duluth and Superior, Wisconsin. Five years after the Civil War, Duluth was America's fastest-growing town. Growth has slowed at this "Zenith City on the Unsalted Sea," but Minnesota's third largest municipality continues to fascinate as it deals with changing weather, capricious economics, and, above all, North America's largest natural wonder.

There's plenty to do here, in all climates. Summer evenings can be spent watching minor-league baseball as the Duluth-Superior Dukes take on teams from Fargo, Lincoln, St. Paul, and Winnipeg. Or, head downtown to the sand spit called Canal Park and do the Lakewalk, a paved pathway with sweeping views of the city over one shoulder and the lake all around. Look, too, for the S.S. *William A. Irvin* Ore Boat Museum and the North Shore Scenic Railroad. By all means, get out on the lake, whether on a harbor cruise or in a canoe, a kayak, a sailboat, or as part of a fishing charter.

When the weather turns cold, try the cross-country ski trails, the snowmobile trails, or, because no one can stay off the lake, a day of ice fishing. The city has a rich collection of public and private art museums. A good place to begin is the Tweed Museum of Art. When temperatures drop through zero, curl up with a good book from one of four locally owned, independent bookstores. No matter the weather, there are at least four worthy, beer-oriented sites in what is good-naturedly called the Finnish Riviera.

(For more information, call the Visitors Bureau toll-free at (800) 438-5884, or check the Duluth Convention and Visitors Bureau Web site, www.visitduluth.com, or the Greater Downtown Council Web site, www.downtownduluth.com.)

Fitger's Brewhouse, Brewery and Grille

600 E. Superior St.
Duluth, MN 55802
Telephone: (218) 726-1392
Web site: www.brewhouse.net
Hours: 11 a.m.-1 a.m. Monday-Saturday, 11 a.m.-midnight Sunday (bar); 11 a.m.-10 p.m. Sunday-Wednesday and 11 a.m.-11 p.m. Thursday-Saturday (kitchen). Closed New Year's Day, Thanksgiving, and Christmas.
Nearby attraction: Lake Superior, one block east.

Next to running out of ingredients, the worst thing that can happen to a brewing operation is a fire. In updating the brewmaking equipment in the spring of 2001, that is exactly what took place at Fitger's. The owners quickly installed not just any tap beer but some of the best taps available. Customers could choose from three Lake Superior Brewing Company ales, plus such stalwarts as Beamish Irish Stout, Pyramid Heffeweisen, Black Dog Honey Raspberry, Gulden Draak Ale, Three Floyds Alpha King, and central Minnesota's very own Schell's Pils.

Despite such an all-star lineup, regulars were pleased when, a couple of months later, they could once again order refreshment made on the premises. Fitger's currently offers seven brews, among them:

• **Lighthouse Ale,** a golden liquid made with American and Czech hops.

Fitger's Brewhouse, Brewery and Grille, Duluth.

• **El Nino India Pale Ale**, which is aged in oak.

• **Witchtree Extra Special Bitter**, made with English hops and malt.

• **Big Boat Oatmeal Stout**, which is a dark and complex brew.

Look for a featured brew, a seasonal fruit, and a brewer's choice from among a total of twenty seasonal beers and ales. Among the more intriguing are fruit beers, which may feature apples, apricots, blueberries, raspberries, cranberries, or pumpkin, depending on the time of year and the brewers' inclination. Also on tap is Delirium Tremens, an ale made in Belgium; it is served only in ten-ounce glasses and contains an intimidating 8.5 percent alcohol. Microbottled products include Anchor Steam, Black Dog Honey Raspberry, Schell's Pils, and Summit Extra Pale Ale. A dozen wines are featured, hard apple cider can be had on tap, and Fitger's own Driftwood Draft Root Beer is popular.

Besides detailing a range of edibles, the menu carefully explains the brewing process. Something like connect-the-dots for grownups, customers are shown and told about everything from original gravity to the importance of nitrogen content. Popular food items range from eight distinct hamburgers to Philly steak and turkey cobb sandwiches. There are other sandwiches, four kinds of quesadillas, eight different salads, vegetarian black-bean chili, and desserts on the menu. The menu also pitches the brewery's souvenir T-shirts, caps, mugs, and other items.

BEER & TAVERN-RELATED
Web sites

Many Minnesota taverns have their own Web sites. Look for the sites at the top of each tavern review in this book. To learn more about drinks and destinations in general, check out these Internet locales.

- **www.alestreetnews.com** News, features, tours, events, etc., aimed at recruiting subscribers to *Ale Street News*, a print publication covering the Northeastern United States.

- **www.allaboutbeer.com** Promotes *All About Beer* magazine with news, features, and directories.

- **www.beer.com** Apparently a site for those who have just turned 21, beer.com offers lots of girls, music, glitz, noise, and "shameless promos."

- **www.beerexpedition.com** This is an exhaustive list of North American breweries.

- **www.beerhistory.com** Just what it says—a thorough, clever, and enjoyable history.

- **www.beerhunter.com** Englishperson Michael Jackson (not the guy who dances backward) teaches us all about beer on his never-ending quest.

- **www.breweriana.com** All those items that looked so good to you in taverns (signs, trays, cans, bottles, more) can now be in your own home—for a price.

- **www.realbeer.com** Calling itself "the beer portal," this site has something for everyone, though the bar and brewpub listings for Minnesota are a bit dated.

Fitger's offers live music Fridays and Saturdays, a Grateful Dead bootleg night Mondays, live jazz Wednesday evenings, and rare and obscure recorded rock music Thursdays in an atmosphere dubbed the Starfire Lounge. Weekend musicians might be Azure DeJour, Erik from the Urban Hillbilly Quartet, or groups such as Spoon-Plug or Urban Renewal Bluegrass. Music nights are good nights to get to know the natives.

Weekly drink specials are many and varied. Happy hours, 3-6 p.m. Monday-Friday, and 8-9 p.m. Monday-Thursday, offer $2 pints. A happy hour for foodies, also 3-6 p.m. Monday-Friday, knocks a dollar off the price of any appetizer. Monday's bottle special stars microbrewed beer from around the world; Lake Superior Brewing Company products are in the spotlight Tuesday; from 9 p.m. to midnight Thursday, count on $3-$5 off a pitcher.

All of this is encased in the Fitger's complex, which has an upscale hotel on one end and retail shops on the other. The atmospheric old ironstone building is only a block or two from the original Fitger's brewery, where strong beer was brewed from 1857 to 1972. The present incarnation of the brewery opened for business in 1995 and, except for a period after the 2001 blaze, has been brewing ever since.

Grandma's Saloon & Grill

522 S. Lake Ave.
Duluth, MN 55802
Telephone: (218) 727-4192
Web site: www.grandmasrestaurants.com
Hours: 11 a.m.-1 a.m. daily (summer); 11:30 a.m.-1 a.m. Monday-Friday, 11 a.m.-1 a.m. Saturday-Sunday (winter); kitchen closes 10:30 p.m. summer, 10 p.m. winter.
Nearby attraction: The aerial lift bridge, one block east.

Grandma's—and many of the places making up Duluth nightlife—is on a narrow extension of land running east from Interstate 35 and the Duluth downtown. The restaurants, bars, and clubs jut into Lake Superior and can be located by keeping an eye out for the aerial lift bridge. The venerable silver structure, as the name suggests, elevates its entire floor so that large Lake Superior freighters and other craft can move between the Duluth Harbor Basin and the mighty lake.

One of the neat things about Grandma's, it turns out, is that a drinker or diner can sit inside or out and take in the bridge as it is put through its paces. There are other aspects to Grandma's, not the least of which is that it sponsors

Grandma's Saloon & Grill, beneath the aerial lift bridge, Duluth.

one of the dozen most popular marathons in the country. Each September since 1976, runners have departed Two Harbors and run along the coast a ways, covering 26.2 miles to finish at this watering hole.

Initially, Grandma's was a small and modest place. It has grown, along with the race, so that now it has two floors and a deck, seating a total of six hundred. (There are other Grandma locations, too, both here, in the Twin Cities, and in Fargo, South Dakota.) Whether sitting and watching the bridge work or running a ghastly distance, customers can sample what Grandma's offers.

Assuming no one wants a macrobrew on tap, check out Bass Ale, Newcastle Ale, Guinness, a seasonal offering or two, and Grandma's Trusty Old Brew, made by the Lake Superior Brewing Company across town. This also is one of Leinenkugel's largest accounts. The Chippewa Falls, Wisconsin, brewer, recently acquired by Miller Brewing (and, therefore, Philip Morris), displays the familiar canoe-shaped tap handles upstairs and down. There are several other domestic and imported bottled brews, plus wine and liquor.

The second floor seems to be more of a sports bar, whereas the first floor is committed to serious food and drink. Popular luncheon fare includes steak sandwiches, French dip, and good-sized burgers. Later on, order such better-than-bar meals as chicken Tetrazzini. In the summer, the three kitchens run simultaneously.

The second-floor jukebox offers a good selection of rock music but is fed money only sporadically. Several TV sets flash golf or baseball or whatever is in season, but the employees here wisely dial the collective audio to zero. While the deck is the best place to see the bridge do tricks, the span also is eminently visible from the second floor.

Grandma's has an ambitious souvenir shop just beyond the main entrance. Besides apparel, such items as salsas and other food enhancers are displayed. Across Lake Street is an even larger shop housing Grandma's trinkets. Everything from glassware to chocolates, film, and post cards fills the windows.

Lake Superior Brewing Company

2711 W. Superior St.
Duluth, MN 55806
Telephone: (218) 723-4000
Web site: www.lakesuperiorbrewing.com
Hours: Normal business hours; call for tour information.
Nearby attraction: Jay Cooke State Park.

Lake Superior Brewing Company began it all in December 1994, brewing small batches of hearty ale in space rented in the Fitger's complex. The microbrewery moved to its current, red brick address in 1998, where head brewer Dale Kleinschmidt maintains a 4,000-barrel capacity that incorporates refurbished dairy equipment, among other plumbing, to produce four year-round ales and at least four seasonals. One of the seasonals, Old Man Winter Warmer, also is bottled.

Kleinschmidt does not call himself a brewmaster. Humbly, he says he is a home brewer who got bigger and better after briefly opening a storefront homebrew shop. He and others produce Special Ale, Mesabi Red, Kayak Kolsche, and Sir Duluth Oatmeal Stout, on tap and in bottles. The seasonals vary, from a wheat beer to an India pale ale. Mesabi Red, an American dark-red ale, is the most alcoholic at 6.5 percent. For kids and designated drivers, there is High Bridge Root Beer, with a tantalizing aftertaste of wintergreen. Lake Superior water is used in every product.

Special Ale is the microbrewery's most popular brew, and with good reason. It is a flavorful, American-style British pale ale that has been favorably reviewed by a number of national and international beer-drinking experts. One or more Lake Superior products can be found on tap from south of the Twin

Cities to the Canadian border in eastern Minnesota. To get an up-close look at the brewing process, give Dale a call. Tours are given free of charge during the week and, occasionally, on weekends if the group is large and eager.

As for directions, Superior Street runs west of and parallel to Interstate 35. It is the main street running southwest to northeast. The brewery is in a commercial-industrial area south of the downtown.

Sir Benedict's Tavern on the Lake

805 E. Superior St.
Duluth, MN 55802
Telephone: (218) 728-1192
Web site: www.sirbenedicts.com
Hours: 11 a.m.-11 p.m. Monday-Tuesday, 11 a.m.-1 a.m. Wednesday-Saturday, 11 a.m.-11 p.m. Sunday. Closed New Year's Day, Easter, Thanksgiving, Christmas Day.
Nearby attraction: Chester Park, with an elevated lake view, is a few blocks northwest.

Here's a vote for Sir Benedict's Tavern being the best possible use of a defunct gas station. The cream-colored structure a few blocks north of Fitger's is easy to spot—the Union Jack and the Stars and Stripes flutter in the Lake Superior wind above it. Below, visitors will find the most varied beer and ale selection anywhere in the state's third-largest city.

Nine taps offer Beamish Stout, Coors Light, Hardcore Cider, Killian's Red, Lake Superior Special Ale, Leinenkugel's Berry Weiss, Leinenkugel's Honey Weiss, Samuel Adams, and Summit Great Northern Porter. Stored below are 160 bottles of brews from all over the world, though the selection leans toward English beer and ale. For designated drivers there are 25 kinds of soft drinks.

Sir Benedict's is neither large nor pretentious. Nevertheless, the place is repeatedly named by the local alternative weekly to have the best beer selection and the best sandwiches in Duluth. In fact, before other taverns caught on to the value of serving good food, this was virtually the only tavern where packaged and portioned food was not the norm.

Steve, the manager, says the Sir Melt, a patty melt with a little something extra, is extremely popular. So are the veggie melt and the turkey sandwich. The soups and salads are worth sampling, too. Hardy types can take their food and drink on the small patio that faces the lake. (What is it about far-north

Sir Benedict's Tavern on the Lake, Duluth.

bistros and outside dining? Even in the summer, flatlanders will cringe inside at the bar on any evening when there is an offshore breeze.)

Music is a nightly event, involving blues, folk, jazz, or Celtic tunes. Patrons are of several types. They include fans of whatever musicians are scheduled, beer connoisseurs, downtown merchants headed home to one of the string of nice houses, old and new, that run along the shoreline, a few college-age kids, and somebody from, say, Colorado who happened to be in the vicinity and learned of the pub on a Web site. Neither jukebox nor elevator music intrudes on conversation, and happy hour, with discounted drafts, runs 4-7 p.m.

The folks who work here show their sense of humor on at least an annual basis. During the sled dog races in February, Sir Benedict's holds the Dog Days of Winter Folk Fest. Patrons are given the opportunity to hear some good acoustic tunes as they sip suds named after dogs. The bow-wow beers are offered at special prices.

GRAND MARAIS

Lots of places in Minnesota feel like jumping-off points, but none more than this Lake Superior village of 1,237, populated by retirees, artists and artisans, backpackers, and folks running tourism-related businesses.

Driving here from Duluth, an out-of-state resident stumbles on one of the great vacation values in all of the Gopher State. There are seven state parks between Duluth and the U.S.-Canadian border; a $4 charge at the first park admits the keeper of his or her stub to every other park he/she can visit in the same day.

And what parks! Gooseberry Falls, the southernmost, thunders down out of the hills and into the big lake in a series of leaps and swooshes. Each of the others has the intoxicating aroma of pine and iron-flecked water, and the ability to convince the viewer that America isn't yet overrun with malls and fast-food joints.

Grand Marais is a placid place, ideal for loading up for a trip up the Gun Flint Trail (Highway 12, just outside of town) and into the Boundary Waters Canoe Area. For more information, call (888) 922-5000, or try the Grand Marais Visitor Center Web site, www.grandmaraismn.com, or www.northshorevisitor.com.

Gun Flint Tavern

111 Wisconsin Street
Grand Marais, MN 55604
Telephone: (218) 387-1563
Web site: www.gunflinttavern.com
Hours: 11:30 a.m.-midnight Monday-Thursday; 11:30 a.m.-1 a.m. Friday-Saturday; noon-midnight Sunday. Closed Christmas Day.
Nearby attraction: Eagle Mountain, highest point (2,301 ft.) in Minnesota, ten miles west.

The Gun Flint Tavern opened its doors in May 1998, because when Susan and Jeff left home and drove down the Gun Flint Trail to town, they had no place to hang out. So the two of them leased the former bank building facing Harbor Park and Lake Superior, converted the vault into a beer cooler, and awaited customers. The customers came, and many have returned.

Beer drinkers show up for the dozen or so tap beers and ales. In alphabetical order, look for Bass Ale, Blue Moon, Deer Brand, Goose Island Honkers Ale, Guinness, Harp, Summit Maibock Lager, and five brews crafted by the Lake Superior Brewing Company of Duluth. The drafts are supplemented by a large number of bottles, none of which ever bobbed by the thousands down a huge brewery line. They range from Apricot Ale to Mike's Hard Lemonade.

The bar seats about ten patrons and tables accommodate just over twice that many. On a fall visit one afternoon, a couple of guys were playing chess, several people were dining, and at least one alleged beer devotee was studying the various pump handles. Blessedly, the Gun Flint is a nonsmoking venue. Long may it wave!

Besides the beer, folks gravitate here for the food. Susan has two decades of experience turning out flavorful stuff for other restaurants, and now she is showing what she can do on her own. Favorites include several different soups, a tamale dinner, a chicken mole dinner, wild mushroom tarragon, smoked fish, an occasional pizza, and an array of grilled sandwiches.

This is a funky place in the very best sense of the word. The creepiest, most obvious tourist is treated with all the respect accorded a native retiree or a merchant. No jukebox intrudes on the calm, which is enhanced by soft blues programming delivered via satellite. Blues or jazz musicians hold forth live on weekend evenings.

Off season, try the 8-10 p.m. happy hour, where 50 cents is deducted from each pint. Several decent wines also are available, as are souvenir caps, T-shirts, sweatshirts, bar glasses, and coffee mugs. Grand Marais has artsy pretensions, and some of the regulars are professional or amateur artists.

Those who want to walk around town can score a decent pizza one block north. Or, if they are feeling like Homer Simpson, they can down a beer here and then hike less than two blocks to a place that modestly says it makes "the world's best donuts." On the other hand, it's a treat to be seated at the bar, brew in hand, waiting for Susan to do a better culinary thing than anyone has a right to expect this far from what passes for civilization.

MINNESOTA'S
10 best places

Arranged in no particular order, here are some great places to see prior to retreating to a tavern and finding out if everyone else liked the attractions as well as you did.

1. Minneapolis Sculpture Garden. The big spoon with the cherry in it is as clever a piece of public art as a traveler is apt to run across. And it's within a couple of miles of several Uptown taverns!

2. Minnesota State Fair, St. Paul. In something of a no-man's land, tavern-wise, the fair and its grounds are enough to make even the most cynical believe that there is a near-perfect America out there somewhere.

3. New York Mills. Wholesome farm life meets Bohemia in a part of the state the unsuspecting might dismiss.

4. Lake Superior, as seen from the lofty I-35 wayside just south of Duluth. Nothing else, not the Grand Canyon, not the Great Wall of China, is as impressive as the big, silent lake. Superior also is visible from a couple of Duluth taverns.

5. Vermilion Lake. Large enough to have an island for every day of the year, Vermilion is fortunate to be a wonderful, unspoiled lake with several classic resorts.

6. The Gunflint Trail, Superior National Forest. A must drive for anyone who believes that all the wild places have been tamed.

7. Gooseberry Falls State Park. If you tire of looking at the falls, Lake Superior is just over your shoulder. And there's a small town with the impossibly exotic name of Castle Danger nearby. A close second might be the tumbling Big Fork River in the vicinity of Big Falls.

8. The Spam Museum, Austin. Need we say more?

9. Detroit Lakes. Maybe because it was a perfect day when we visited, we found the village and the lakeshore picture-perfect.

10. Fourth Street, Northeast or Southeast, in Minneapolis. A street only Bob Dylan could (and did) love. Positively.

GRAND RAPIDS

The term "mill town" may evoke a negative image—grimy, depressed—and depressing—housing, labor unrest, dying industry, and dead-end lives. Grand Rapids is a mill town, and it is the exception to the rule. Paper is milled here on the banks of the Mississippi River. Not only the big mill itself, but the water, the air, and this progressive town of 8,729 residents are all quite pristine.

Most visitors arrive in the summer to take advantage of the area's many lakes. On a map, Grand Rapids looks as if it were absolutely spattered with blue water in all sizes and shapes. Resorts in Itasca County are a dime a dozen, catering to families who like to swim, fish, sail, or watch the aurora borealis flutter across the northern sky on a midsummer midnight. The resorts hereabouts are exactly the kinds of places that lodge in a kid's memory when he or she thinks of taking off for a week or two with Mom, Dad, Junior, and Sis.

The town itself is a popular place for folks to visit on the occasional rainy day, or to stock up on groceries before heading out to a cottage or cabin. The birthplace of Judy Garland, Grand Rapids offers a range of annual events, from concerts in the performing arts center to the county fair. The former Central School building is an artsy marketplace, there is the Children's Discovery Museum, and the Taconite Trail for bikes begins here.

(For more information, dial (800) GRANDMN, or check these Web sites: www.grandmn.com or northwoodsminnesota.com.)

Forest Lake Restaurant and Lounge

1201 North West 4th Street (Highway 2 West)
Grand Rapids, MN 55744
Telephone: (218) 326-3423
Hours: 11 a.m.-1 a.m. (bar); 7 a.m.-10 p.m. (kitchen). Closed Thanksgiving and Christmas.
Nearby attraction: One thousand area lakes.

Named for the body of water immediately behind it, Forest Lake Restaurant and Lounge certainly looks like it belongs in northern Minnesota. Constructed of western lodge-pole pine in 1980, and with the cedar-sided lounge added a bit later, the destination is popular with locals and with folks passing through on the U. S. highway.

The first decision a visitor will have to make once inside is whether to angle right for the lounge or straight ahead for the restaurant. Opting for the lounge, he or she will find three kinds of Michelob on tap and a number of bottled beers, some of them imported. Liquor also is available, a souvenir hunter can purchase a hat, and music arrives via satellite. Happy hour is a 4:30-6 p.m. Monday-Friday affair.

The lounge menu is a slightly less ambitious version of the restaurant's list. The biggest hit in the tavern may well be a half-pound Bar Burger. Combined with a beer and the usual toppings, it is a meal in itself. The restaurant's most popular meals include the Forest Lake Scrambler for breakfast (eggs, ham, and cheese, served with toast and hash browns); chicken stir fry for lunch; and a nice selection of barbecued ribs and steaks in the evening.

The best time to meet Grand Rapids residents in the bar is during happy hour or on either Friday or Saturday night. The weekday folks look to be a bit older than the weekend drinkers, though there is a nice range of ages on Fridays and Saturdays. Regardless, patrons tend to be nicely tanned in the summer and well insulated in snowmobile suits in the winter. How much more Minnesota can you get?

HIBBING

To every baby boomer, Hibbing first and foremost is the place where Bob Dylan grew up. While Dad ran the hardware store, young Bob Zimmerman envisioned a utopian world while he schemed to leave town. That may be co-incidental, because another American icon, the Greyhound bus, was conceived here. Greyhound, which is all about leaving town, was started by a couple of enterprising fellows who provided cheap transportation among the small towns across the iron range.

The entire municipality was moved, buildings and all, in three separate efforts that began in 1912 and ended in 1934. It seems that the Oliver Mining Company owned the mineral rights beneath the town, and what started with the relocation of a few houses ended with every building adjusted southward, all in search of high-grade iron ore. The public library was the last structure to go.

Plateaus of mine tailings surround this city of 18,046. The color of dried blood, these huge, flat-topped mounds can be seen from various spots on the 40-mile Circle T Bike Trail, part of Minnesota's ambitious rails-to-trails program. If shopping is more your sport, downtown Hibbing has a respectable quantity and quality of retail outlets. It is the kind of place that seems quite pleasant to a vacationer but might well annoy a young troubadour eager to hit the road.

For more information, telephone (800) 4-HIBBING, or contact these Web sites: www.irontrai.org or www.hibbingmn.com.

Atrium Restaurant & Zimmy's Grill

531 E. Howard St.
Hibbing, MN 55746
Telephone: (218) 262-6145
Web site: www.zimmy's.com
Hours: 11 a.m.-1 a.m. (bar), 11 a.m.-8 p.m. Sunday-Tuesday
and 11 a.m.-9 p.m. Wednesday-Saturday (kitchen). Closed
Thanksgiving and Christmas.
Nearby attraction: Minnesota Museum of Mining,
Chisholm.

As a traveler might suspect, the bar/grill side of this downtown site is a tribute to Bob Dylan, who was born a Zimmerman in Duluth before moving with
his family to Hibbing as a small boy. There are Dylan tunes on the jukebox,
album covers and other mementos on the walls, and several decent beers on
tap. Leinenkugel's Creamy Dark and Honey Weiss are available, as are Labatt's
Ice and three different varieties of light beer. Imported bottles include Corona,
Guinness, and Heineken.

Atrium Restaurant & Zimmy's Grill, Hibbing.

Happy hour is at 4-6 p.m. Monday-Friday. This works well for folks who have come to dinner, since they can remain in the bar for fare such as the double cheeseburger or walk a few paces into the restaurant for a more extensive menu. Favorites in the evening range from steaks to chimichangas to pizza, while the headliner on the separate lunch menu is an Oriental chicken salad with a side of wild rice soup. This is a venue for many special events, including high school reunions. Then, and just about only then, is the music live. That might change, should Mr. Dylan ever come back to town.

The bar and restaurant also have something of a history, at least locally. Trolley cars were housed here in the early 1900s. A few years later, a succession of service stations took up the space. The restaurant is almost twenty years old. Its history is encased in several photos lining the northeast wall, on the far side of the apple tree that stretches toward the large skylight. Both destinations offer mostly local folks, but visitors from all fifty states and several foreign countries have arrived to pay their respects to one of the twentieth century's most widely known entertainers.

A nice time to hit this pleasant tavern is after dark Tuesday, for a couple of reasons. That is Tap Beer (discount) Night and is otherwise a rather subdued evening. If you ask, perhaps the barkeep or an employee will show you the battered Los Angeles Lakers hat bearing Bob Dylan's autograph. For the record, there is no official connection between the singer/songwriter and the bar. As a matter of fact, there is only one Zimmerman remaining in the Hibbing telephone book.

INTERNATIONAL FALLS

To paraphrase the old Fabulous Thunderbirds song, the motto of International Falls should be, "Got cold if you want it." This small (population 7,638) town on the Canadian border frequently displays the lowest temperature in the 48 states. That may be a bum rap, however, since the coldest temperature ever recorded in Minnesota was -59 F degrees at Leech Lake Dam in 1899 and again at Pokegama Falls in 1903.

Nevertheless, the temps generated here are not the bogus wind chills but are instead the real thing. Why does the Gopher State get cold enough to freeze a gopher? Students of climate and/or geography know that the center of a continent is always chillier than the coasts. Any map of North America will show Minnesota to be a long way from either ocean.

Yet one of the remarkable things about Minnesotans is their willingness to enjoy this expansive state year round. An out-of-state friend was visiting his college-age daughter on a January day that could only be described as beyond cold. While the sky was cloudless, the noontime temperature was no more than -20 F degrees. As father and daughter warmed up in a lakeside restaurant, they glanced through a wide window. Out on the ice, kids and adults had created a quarter-mile track. They were roaring around the oval on dirt bikes with studded tires, beneath a wan winter sun, fighting a wind chill that their activity increased!

Fight the chill long enough to look around International Falls. A good view of Canada is difficult, due to the big paper mill on the Rainy River bank. Instead, check out the giant thermometer in Smoky Bear Park before buying supplies for a voyage onto huge Rainy Lake or a visit to Voyageurs National Park, the west end of which is only seven miles east of town.

Rumors Up North

International Mall
1925 Valley Pine Circle
International Falls, MN 56649
Telephone: (218) 283-2868
Hours: 11 a. m.-1 a. m. Closed major holidays.
Nearby attraction: Voyageurs National Park, seven miles east on Highway 11.

An occupant of a Rumors barstool emptied his glass and said to another: "I tell you, it got cold out at my place last night."

His fellow imbiber went for the bait. "How cold did it get?"

"It got down below Bemidji!" The jokester laughed at least as hard as his audience at the punch line.

A locally popular tavern in the International Mall, Rumors doesn't really heat up until the climate cools. Residents appreciate their short summers and spend every spare moment on the area's 84,000 acres of water. Once it turns cold—and it does so with alacrity—locals show up at Rumors to talk about ice fishing, the fish they caught, and the fish that got away. They are big snowmobilers, too, as the sign outside the front door indicates: patrons are admonished not to park their machines on the sidewalk.

This is a working person's place to relax. There are games, from foosball to air hockey to darts. The only beer on tap is Budweiser, and except for maybe a Corona, a visitor would be hard pressed to find anything foreign. That's right, though International Falls is separated only by the Rainy River from Canada, there are no Canadian beers here. Forget about ordering any of your favorite brews and instead bend a macrobrew elbow with a regular patron.

Rumors sits in the shadow of a large and growing Menard's store. The bar offers appetizers and a jukebox that features rock, old and new, and country. Not the place to discuss politics or the role of hops in making beer, it is instead a fine source for getting tipped to where the fishing is best, which snowmobile trails to take, and, most of all, how cold it gets here in "the nation's ice box."

Rosie, the owner and bartender, will discount beer during happy hour, 6-7 p.m., and peddle a souvenir T-shirt, sweatshirt, or cap. She is also the person who schedules occasional disc jockey, karaoke, or live band performances. The parking lot, on a winter evening, is a mix of cars, pickups, and snowmobiles.

Perhaps the attitude of Rumors and of the town itself is best expressed by a sign in front of Rainy River Community College, just across the street. It reads: "Books are mandatory, fishing rod is optional." Not a bad motto, especially around here.

KINNEY

The main highway—and virtually everthing else—bypasses Kinney these days. Once a burgeoning town of more than 2,000 residents, there are now only 234 people here, and many of them are retired or otherwise not working. Located in the middle of the Mesabi Iron Range, this village probably reached its zenith around 1951, the year Minnesota iron hit peak production. By the late 1950s, most of the high-grade ore had been mined. In 1967, low-grade taconite pellets exceeded shipments of more valuable ore. In all, good times on the Mesabi Range lasted about seventy years.

(The highway serving Kinney is a state road, 169, running between Virginia and Chisholm.)

Mary's Bar

401 Main St.
Kinney, MN 55758
Telephone: (218) 258-2211
Hours: 1-11 p.m. or when the crowd thins.
Closed most holidays.
Nearby attraction: Iron Range Interpretative Center, Highway 169, Chisholm.

Mary's Bar is the only business still open in Kinney. Midway between Hibbing and Virginia and just north of Highway 169, the town is surrounded by mine tailings and by gaping, open-pit mines that are now filled with water. "It doesn't look so bad when there's lots of snow," an area resident said apologetically.

The tavern is as modest as the town. There is a Grain Belt beer sign above the entrance, but except for Miller and Anheuser-Busch products, there is not much to drink. Mary, a Chisholm native whose maiden name was Poplovich and who married an Anderson, lives next door in a mobile home. She is eighty-six and shows up at the bar only when her back isn't killing her. Despite all that, she remains an activist for what once was as nice a little burg as a visitor was apt to find across the vast, lake- and tree-dotted rangeland.

Mary's Bar, Kinney.

"Once there were two schools here," she says. "They were nice, too. They had real marble floors. Why they were closed I do not know. This was a much better town when the mines were open. We had grocery stores, a candy store, a movie ..."

One of seven children, Mary watched her Serbian-American father go to work every day in the mines. Her husband is dead and her children now live in Missouri and North Dakota. A long-time Kinney booster, she reports with indignation that the once-proud municipality had to obtain federal aid a few years back so the streets could be repaired. The bar evidently has stayed open because local residents need a rallying point.

"I never charge for wedding receptions," she says. "They only pay for what they drink."

Small and tidy, the tavern shines with a vinyl floor and eight or ten stools plus a few tables. Prices are moderate and there are always a couple of fellows at the bar, to the right of the front door. More often than not, they worked in mines here or nearby.

Ken, the bartender, sells canned or bottled beer or liquor on site only. Should you stop, inquire about Mary's health. Maybe he will suggest you go next door and learn a few things from Kinney's only remaining retailer.

ROSEAU

Winter, summer, or anywhere in between, a visitor quickly learns that Roseau is the home of Polaris, a leading maker of off-road vehicles. But for the hospital, the ball fields, Messiah Church, and a dozen or so downtown blocks, snowmobiles and all-terrain vehicles are permitted anywhere (such as the golf course—with caution). There are routes for these work and recreational conveyances around and through town. All a visitor has to do to score a ride is to make friends with a resident.

That can be accomplished by knowing a little something about local hockey. Roseau has won six boys' high school hockey state championships, most recently in 1999. Every boy (and numerous girls) appears to be on the ice, with a stick, from fall into spring. Depending on whom you meet in this town of 2,755, they will report that the tavern detailed next is either 29 or 67 steps away from the hockey arena. The number of steps must be related to the degree of thirst! Moms and dads dash to the tavern and back after each of hockey's three periods. When there is snow on the ground, which is rather often, the path between the venues is easy to find and follow.

For more information, call the Roseau Tourism Bureau at (800) 815-1824, or go to http://city.roseau.mn.us/.

American Legion Post 24

321 N. Main Ave.
Roseau, MN 56757
Telephone: (218) 463-3681
Hours: 2 p.m.-1 a.m. (bar); 5-9:30 p.m. (kitchen).
Closed Easter, Thanksgiving, and Christmas.
Nearby attraction: Agassiz National Wildlife Refuge, 40 miles south of town, then west off Highway 89.

American Legion Post 24 in Roseau.

In any given Minnesota town, the most popular spot for a beer and a conversation is apt to be the American Legion Post. In Roseau, Post No. 24 is a fine example, situated just north of the business district, in the shadow of the hockey arena. Unlike some other taverns in this book, locals always greatly outnumber anyone else.

Legion posts are not frantic about décor or advertising, and they may appear to be off limits to non-Legion members. In small towns, however, the posts usually need and welcome anyone of legal drinking age. To enjoy themselves here, all visitors have to do is sign a guest book. There are no obligations or charges except for whatever they consume.

Budweiser and Bud Light are the only tap alternatives, but there are several bottled-beer selections, and liquor is available. Happy hour is 4-5 p.m. The bar here is up half a flight of stairs. Half a flight down is the dining room, where favorite meals such as steak and walleye are served. Bar food includes appetizers and burgers. The jukebox has a little bit of everything—rock, country, polka, ballads. Bands show up mostly on weekend evenings.

Visit a Legion post to learn a bit of whimsy or gossip or solid, insider information about the community. For instance, one of the busiest times at the post is during the Roseau County Fair, which takes place in July. Besides the fairgoers and exhibitors, lots of kids attend a summer hockey school. Their parents have been known to kill time happily here.

One occupant of a barstool noted that the most popular Web site is www.roseaurams.com. It proves, he contended, that the Roseau Rams high school boys' hockey squad is superior to Warroad as a producer of hockey players, and that the boys and girls featured on the site represent all that is good about chasing a puck up and down the ice. Surrounded by Roseau residents, only a most imprudent person or a diehard Warroad backer would dare to disagree.

THIEF RIVER FALLS

Virtually 300 miles northwest of the Twin Cities and even a few miles north of Fargo, Thief River Falls nevertheless seems to be a livable, small (pop. 8,484) town. The terrain is flat in the extreme and fairly treeless, yet the municipality is an oasis of shade in warm weather. In cold weather, there is little in the countryside except occasional farmsteads to stop the wind and snow. Could there have been trees at one time? The Convention and Visitors Bureau handout says the place was developed along with lumber milling in 1887.

Today, there are 21 parks near where two rivers, the Thief River and the Red Lake River, meet. Some 7.3 miles of walking paths connect several parks. Speaking of trails, folks wait for winter to aim their Arctic Cats along 500 local miles of groomed pathways. Birders will be rewarded with a visit, as a wide variety of waterfowl and other birds stop here on their migration routes. They are in the area to frequent the lush tallgrass prairies, which are dotted with islands of aspen, balsam, and poplar.

(For additional information, call the Convention and Visitors Bureau at (800) 827-1629 or (218) 681-3720, or try this Web site: www.ci.thief-river-falls.mn.us.)

Black Cat Sports Bar & Grill

1080 Highway 32 South
Thief River Falls, MN 56701
Telephone: (218) 681-8910
Hours: 11 a.m.-1:30 a.m. (bar); 11 a.m.-10:30 p.m. (kitchen). Closed New Year's Day, Thanksgiving, and Christmas.
Nearby attraction: Old Mill State Park, 30 miles northwest, off Highway 59.

Right off the bat, to use a sports metaphor, visitors might as well know that this is a sports bar. Having said that, it should be added that the Black Cat is like no other sports bar they are likely to encounter. Separated from the Arctic Cat snowmobile plant and test grounds by a state highway, this modern tav-

The Black Cat Sports Bar & Grill, Thief River Falls.

ern with a woodsy look to it salutes snowmobilers and drivers of all-terrain vehicles. It is no coincidence that Arctic Cat produces large numbers of both.

Even better, daylight patrons can go to the front window and watch factory riders and drivers testing the latest products on terrain that is rugged in warm weather and snowy in cold. Turning away from the proving grounds view, folks can wander the perimeter of the Black Cat, learning something of the history and heritage of snowmobiling. Don't look for Derek Jeter or Randy Moss in the framed portraits; rather, these are pictures of warmly dressed guys who have just won a long and arduous race across ice and snow. There are also some neat memorabilia from the Arctic Cat plant. (The restaurant is also listed as a museum in the annual visitors' guide.)

The Black Cat audience is a nice mix of Cat employees, other locals, people who motored past and decided to stop, and folks staying the night at the Best Western motel next door. (Both places share a driveway.) Three big beers are on tap: Bud Light, Miller Lite, and Michelob Amber Bock. There is an adequate domestic and foreign bottle selection, and for those who are driving, Schell's 1919 Root Beer can be had on draft. The jukebox offers up everything from speed metal to country, there are a couple of television sets tuned to sports, and souvenirs that include T-shirts, sweatshirts, and hats are available. The bar souvenirs face a lot of competition, however, since many of the natives at the bar and at the tables wear black and lime-green Arctic Cat gear.

Food here includes several interesting items. The cook's name is Slim and she has created the Slimburger, which is very popular. Also available are several other sandwiches, an 8-oz. steak, grilled chicken breast salad, and such great finger foods as Black Cat nachos. There is no discernible happy hour, but that does not stop people from stopping here once their workday is done.

The careful reader with a map of Minnesota at hand will note that a drive of only about an hour—55 miles, to be exact—separates Roseau and the Polaris plant from Thief River Falls and the Arctic Cat facility. Besides the relative merits of the two companies' products, high school hockey is another subject better left alone. From personal experience, however, we can report that telling the bartender a pickup truck in the parking lot was left with its lights on will endear a stranger to the crowd.

WARROAD

Warroad (named after the path taken by battling Chippewa and Sioux), population 1,896, is the only U. S. town of any size on Lake of the Woods. The vast reservoir offers 65,000 miles of shoreline and 14,000 islands, and is fed by the Rainy and other rivers. Ultimately, all of this water reaches Hudson Bay. Minnesota and the provinces of Manitoba and Ontario surround the lake, a fisher's paradise by all accounts. This, too, is the site of America's strangest piece of real estate, the Northwest Angle State Forest.

The angle is a pudgy peninsula attached to the southeast corner of Manitoba, and more than a dozen miles north of anything else in the Lower 48— yet it is considered part of Minnesota. Easily reached from Warroad by boat, the angle can also be approached on wheels by driving out of Warroad six miles north to the border, then following Manitoba roads some 50 circuitous miles northwest and then northeast. An Indian reservation and several fishing camps are found along the angle's bulbous shore, though in truth the province of Ontario, to the east, owns most of the islands and offers the best fishing.

Warroad is the home of Marvin Windows and Christian Brothers Hockeysticks; a cynic might say the former product is made to be broken, while the latter is made to do some breaking. A visit to the tavern described next should convince vacationers of the importance of both industries to this pleasant, farnorth hamlet.

(For more information, contact the Warroad Chamber of Commerce at (800) 328-4455 or (218) 386-3543, or go to this Web site: www.warroad.org.)

Main Street Bar and Grill

118 Main Ave. N. E.
Warroad, MN 56763
Telephone: (218) 386-9955
Hours: 11 a.m.-1 a.m. Closed Sundays and major holidays.
Nearby attraction: Lake of the Woods.

This place is as good as any to meet a mix of Warroad natives and hardy souls preparing to fish Lake of the Woods. Across from the Chamber of Commerce and with a bright green awning, Main Street Bar and Grill offers good food and an adequate supply of beer. The taps house only Budweiser or Bud Light, but there are a couple dozen different brews, including Canadian brands, in the cooler.

The walls are lined with hockey sticks and photos of fellows who have made or are making it as professional hockey players. These Warroad guys are idolized by the locals and at least given a nod of respect by the high school's foes, so only a fool would make disparaging remarks about anything hockey-related. Perhaps a safer subject might be where the fishing is best and how to find it on the vast lake, which begins at the town's front door.

Jackie, who owns this tavern and does the cooking, is rather proud of the menu. There is a nice variety of sandwiches such as patty melts for lunch, while dinner might be anything from chicken Alfredo to quesadillas. Due to its modest size, the grill is readily visible from the bar. A customer will find it encouraging that most stuff appears to be fresh rather than thawed and/or microwaved.

Happy hour takes places 4-6 p.m. Monday-Saturday. That is when a visitor is most apt to meet employees of Marvin Windows, Christian Brothers Hockeysticks, or one or more downtown merchants. Liquor is available, as are souvenir T-shirts and hats. This is a family place, where the bar is usually male dominated, the tables a nice mix of adults and adults with kids, and the jukebox a mixture of both rock and country tunes.

Though it says "Sports Bar" on that green awning, no one will automatically jabber NFL, NBA, or NASCAR. In fact, those who listen to National Public Radio's "Prairie Home Companion" and enjoy the description of the tavern in Lake Wobegone will feel at home here.

CENTRAL
Minnesota

VISITORS and natives alike assume that Minnesota would be nothing without the Twin Cities. Not only is that presumptuous, it is dead wrong. Central Minnesota is, after all, where the three distinct geographical zones—pine forests, hardwood forests, and prairies—are most in evidence. Each is well represented, more here than to the north or south.

The Mississippi is born, undulates, and enlarges here. It is responsible for the growth of a number of towns, despite the fact that the big river is not commercially navigable north of St. Anthony Falls in Minneapolis. The Father of Waters is joined by several smaller rivers and streams as it gathers power for the trip south. That power must be almost palpable, because it evidently helped nurture some of the famous native sons and daughters of this region.

Aviator Charles Lindbergh, author Sinclair Lewis, contemporary writer and entertainer Garrison Keillor, and the late Vice President Hubert H. Humphrey are just a few of the internationally known people who came of age near one or more of the thousands of lakes or dozens of rivers found in an area bounded more or less by the Twin Cities on the south, Duluth on the north, the St. Croix and Mississippi rivers on the east and the Red River on the west.

BRAINERD

This city of 13,150, smack in the middle of the state, provides ample opportunity for outdoor recreation. North of town, in the center of Crow Wing County, are several major bodies of water—Long, Pelican, and Whitefish lakes, and the Crow Wing, Gull, and Mississippi rivers. Many kinds of water sports and fishing expeditions are offered here.

Tourist brochures boast of many golf courses, backing that up with a list of at least thirty within an hour of Brainerd. Sixteen cross-country ski trails, a downhill ski run on the west side of Gull Lake, and 1,200 miles of snowmobile trails make Brainerd and its many resorts a staging area for winter recreation.

Paul Bunyan, cast in concrete, greets young vacationers by name each year in Nisswa, a dozen miles northwest of Brainerd. (For his location and other information, contact the Brainerd Lakes Area Chamber of Commerce, telephone (800) 450-2838, or check this site: www.explorebrainerdlakes.com.)

Green Mill Restaurant and Bar

2115 S. 6th St.
Brainerd, MN 56401
Telephone: (218) 829-4100
Web site: www.greenmill.com
Hours: noon-1 a.m. Monday-Saturday, noon-midnight
Sunday (bar); 7 a.m.-9 p.m. (kitchen).
Closed New Year's Day, Christmas.
Nearby attraction: 3,000 miles of freshwater shoreline in
Crow Wing County.

How many times has a driver motored all day before checking in for the night, only to be disappointed by the motel's cheesy bar and near-empty restaurant? If that experience is familiar, the Green Mill Restaurant and Bar on the south side of Brainerd will be a most pleasant surprise.

Beer devotees will notice immediately that there are sixteen brews on tap. They run the gamut, from the most domesticated domestic through micro-brews and into such exotics as Honker's Ale, a flavorful German product.

Drinkers who frequent this bar will notice that four tap brands disappear every month and are replaced by four new beers. Green Mill Brew, created by the respected Schell Brewery (see under New Ulm), is always available.

Unlike the all-but-vacant facilities mentioned earlier, the Green Mill, located in the Ramada Inn, is well populated, primarily by people who know each other. "We're going to get a number of tourists, so we cater to the locals to be successful," says Michael, the manager.

Toward this end the modern bar offers happy hour from 4 to 6 p.m. Monday-Friday. Domestic pints are $1.50, offshore beers are $2, and Green Mill Brew is but $1.25. Bottled beer, wine, and liquor also are served, and there are complete lunch and dinner menus.

Those who have patronized any of the thirty Green Mills in six states will be familiar with the restaurant's regular or deep-dish gourmet pizzas, plus sandwiches, salads, and pasta varieties. Pizza, a beer's best friend, is created by hand with yeast-activated dough made fresh daily. There is time to order a pint while waiting for a pie—regular pizzas bake for twenty minutes, deep-dish varieties are in the oven twice that long.

Even before they pull up to the restaurant-bar, visitors entering Crow Wing County will notice that the Green Mill name is associated with a local golf tournament, a kids' hockey league, even a drag race. Michael wants to stay in touch with local drinkers and diners, and sponsoring events is as good a way as any.

But back to the Green Mill itself, which began its post-Prohibition life in 1935 as a St. Paul tavern that made pizzas and offered brews. Because customers enjoy variety here, it is impossible to order a boring megabrew, unless your tastes run in that direction. Happily, Brainerd beer drinkers know better.

(The restaurant/motel complex is on Highway 371, about two miles south of Highway 210 and just east of the Mississippi River.)

COLD SPRING

What should travelers do when they run across a tiny town with its very own brewery? Pray that the car breaks down!

Seriously, this is an oft-overlooked area of the state. The source of crystal-clear brewing water and the northeast edge of a part of Minnesota that produces granite and other building stone, southern Stearns County has a couple of nice lakes and is known for the eastern terminus of the Lake Wobegon Regional Trail. The county is the birthplace of aviation immortal Charles Lindbergh, whose preserved boyhood home stands near the Mississippi River on the southwest edge of Little Falls.

Gluek Brewing Company

219 North Red River Avenue
Cold Spring, MN 56320
Telephone: (320) 685-8686
Web site: www.gluek.com
Hours: 9 a.m.-4 p.m. Closed holidays.
Nearby attraction: Lake Wobegon Regional Trail.

Gluek Brewing Company once made popular beers in Minneapolis. Beginning in 1857, the firm crafted German-style brews and delivered them with wagons pulled by Percheron horses. Immediately following the Prohibition hiatus, the federal government forced all of the reopened breweries to get rid of their bars and restaurants. That is why there is an unrelated Gluek Restaurant in Minneapolis today. But why is the brewery now in Cold Spring, a burg of 3,003 souls some 65 miles northwest of the Twin Cities?

The Minneapolis brewery was sold to G. Heileman, the LaCrosse, Wisconsin, brewer, in 1965. Heileman closed the Gluek facility in 1967 and peddled the Gluek brands to the Cold Spring brewery in 1988. Cold Spring went out of business shortly afterward and the Gluek name, atop the Cold Spring facility, was reborn in 1996. So now, there is a renewed connection between the brewery in Cold Spring and the restaurant in Minneapolis.

As it turns out, the marriage between Gluek and the restaurant is a happy one. Gluek Brewing Company prides itself in making beers that go well with food. The restaurant prides itself in offering food that goes well with beer. It is a match made in heaven, though the various Gluek beer brands can be found elsewhere in Minnesota, as well as in North Dakota, South Dakota, and Wisconsin.

These Gluek (pronounced "Glick") brews currently are produced in Cold Spring:

- **Stite.** This beer has been brewed since 1942, when a patent was approved for it. The only Gluek product in a green bottle, Stite is a German lager that is light but has a pronounced flavor. It was initially crafted at the request of World War II veterans, who had acquired a taste for European beers. Some Stite fans swear that the alcohol level is higher than those of most brews, and therefore have dubbed it "Green Lightning."

- **Golden Pilsner.** The flagship brew is said to go with any type of food. It offers minimal bitterness and a mellow hop finish.

- **Doppelbock.** This dark brown beer is full-bodied; it served in the Middle Ages as "liquid bread" during Lent. The color and character, which go well with beef, lamb, or pork, come from roasted malts.

- **Hefe Weiss.** The well-known cloudy beer, weiss is pale and is made from wheat. Often served with a slice of lemon or mixed with fruit syrup or certain cloves.

Gluek Brewing Company, Cold Springs.

- **Honey Bock.** Sweet malts and a drop of honey combine with a malty finish in an amber-brown drink. Enhances underwhelming food flavors.

- **Marzen.** Barley toasted to a reddish hue gives this red-amber beer its distinctive look. Popular with pizza and other spicy entrees.

Tours of the brewery are offered, and visitors are invited to sample the beers at the end of the tours, which take place whenever the brewery is open. Should travelers roll into Cold Spring on Highway 23 later in the day, they can find one or more Gluek products on tap at local emporia, or at an off-premise store. The brewery sells tasteful T-Shirts, denim shirts, and caps.

Because Gluek brews may have been your dad's favorite, and because a number of swank Twin Cities restaurants offer them, the products have a well-earned and enviable reputation.

FERGUS FALLS

On the eastern edge of the prairie pothole region, Fergus Falls (pop. 13,334) is served by Interstate Highway 94 on its northwest run of 240 miles between Minneapolis and Fargo. The seat of Otter Tail County is dotted with small lakes inside and outside the city limits. It is green in warm weather and an attention-getter at other times, what with raw winds and driving snow. Nevertheless, the birds seem to like it: the county recently was said to be the best place in the state for waterfowl hunting. Even pelicans, those seafarers with the underslung beaks, are known to make their seasonal homes in the area.

This is an enterprising place. Rather than awaiting fun, Fergus Falls supports several fests and get-togethers throughout the year. The Frostbite Festival is held in early February, Summer Fest and the Blues and Brews Festival both go off in June, the county fair is in July, there's a classic car show in August, and the Lincoln Avenue Arts Festival takes place Labor Day Weekend. The free and educational Prairie Wetlands Learning Center is south of I-94 on State Route 210.

(For more information, telephone (800) 726-8959, or go to this Web site: www.visitfergusfalls.com.)

Mabel Murphy's

3401 St. Rt. 210
Fergus Falls, MN 56538
Telephone: (218) 739-4406
Web site: www.mabelmurphysmn.com
Hours: 11 a.m.-1 a.m. Mon.-Sat., noon-midnight Sun. (bar); 11 a.m.-10 p.m. Mon.-Thurs.; 11 a.m.-11 p.m. Fri.-Sat.; noon-9 p.m. Sun. (kitchen).
Nearby attraction: Minnesota's first birding trail parallels Highway 59 from Fergus Falls to Thief River Falls.

Everyone who experiences it will admit that the Minneapolis-Fargo run is a long and somewhat boring drive. Not that anyone should drink and drive, but Mabel Murphy's, just off the southbound Highway 210 exit at I-94, might be worth a visit. Look for the cream-colored, Tudor-style stucco building on the east side of the road.

"We have a lot of local people," says Jo, the manager. "And some people drive down here on a regular basis from Fargo."

The out-of-towners do not show up for the tap beers (Budweiser, Michelob, Killian's Red), but rather for the fifty-plus bottled brands, several of them staunchly Irish, that wait patiently behind the bar. Guinness and Harp move briskly here, an equal mix of the two known as a Black and Tan. Local residents and many transients are aware of the variety of bottled brews available.

The restaurant offers steaks, pasta, and seafood, while the bar specializes in lighter fare. Popular bar items include nachos, a prime rib sandwich, barbecued wings, meatballs, Polish sausage with kraut, and ribs. Perhaps because Mabel Murphy's services an interstate clientele, food is available well after dark.

The jukebox features everything from new country to new rock. Darts are popular, karaoke holds forth on a regular basis, and Thursdays are live trivia nights, with prizes. Happy hour takes place 5-7 p.m. weekdays, and hats and T-shirts are available as souvenirs.

Weather permitting, there is an outside dining area. Weather not permitting, there are three separate, wood-burning fireplaces. All in all, Mabel's is a cozy place to help folks move from one side of Minnesota to the other.

HUTCHINSON

History has it that pioneering folk crested a bluff overlooking a handsome river valley and decided to settle in. That was 150 years ago. Today, Hutchinson boasts a population of 13,307, a busy downtown, pleasant residential streets, numerous antique and gift shops, and that memorable river, now named the Crow. For more information, contact the Hutchinson Area Convention and Visitors Bureau by dialing (800) 572-6899, or (320) 587-5252. Or, go to the Internet and find www.hutchinsonchamber.com.

Bavarian Haus Restaurant

36 North Main Street
Hutchinson, MN 55350
Telephone: (320) 587-4560
Hours: 10:30 a.m.-8 p.m. Monday-Wednesday, 10:30 a.m.-9 p.m. Thursday-Saturday. Closed Sunday and holidays.
Nearby attraction: The Crow River and dam.

Minnesota's small-town eating and drinking establishments never cease to amaze us. Behind this ornate, European-style storefront can be found an astonishing 74 different kinds of German bottled beer. Almost as newsworthy, the Bavarian Haus Restaurant has a wide selection of German wines that includes three or four palatable reds.

"Doris is the authentic German cook and Woody is the beer expert," an employee told us cheerfully. The husband-wife team opened for business in the spring of 1992 and has been going strong since. By the time this book sees print, Woody will have a small bar going in the restaurant's middle room. From there he will dispense German draft beer and wine.

With a decade of experience serving the public, Woody has noted that, while diners often seek a wine recommendation, "Everybody likes to choose their own beer." Hence the Bavarian Haus has printed a beer list, which is long and worth reading. Included here, for example, are five different brews with those ceramic-and-wire, lock-over-center, flip tops. The most called-for beer at the moment is Hacker Pschorr.

The food menus are worthy, too. Luncheon highlights include schnitzel schnitte, which is pan-fried veal on German bread with cold potato salad;

49

Bavarian Haus, Hutchinson.

Bavarian frustuck, or farmer's breakfast (sauteed potatoes, onions, ham, and scrambled egg garnished with parsley, tomatoes, pickles, and toast); frickadellen, a German-style hamburger sandwich served with or without cheeses; or a bratwurst plate, with spatzle.

In the evening, pan-fried veal is also offered, this time in that most German of dishes, Wiener schnitzel. Also popular is rouladen, a beef filet wrapped around carrots, onions, bacon, and a pickle. Schwein haxen are pork hocks, a dish that is succulent and tender. These entrees are accompanied by such German stalwarts as spatzle, kraut, and more. Woody rewards those who clean their plates with an addictive winter-apple schnapps, on the house.

Except for soft, Old World background music, there is little that intrudes. A strolling musician appears only occasionally, for special beer- or wine-tasting events (about which you should ask). Souvenir beer glasses are available, and a wider array of glasses and mugs will be offered at the new bar. Diners on weekends include a number of folks from places such as the Twin Cities, 60 miles east on Highway 7, or that Germanic Minnesota town, New Ulm, 40 miles south on Highway 15.

Like the locals on weekdays, weekenders visit the Bavarian Haus because the food is homemade, and because the place is quaint and authentic. Woody says the goals here are high quality and good service, so perhaps a diner's most trying ordeal will be deciding which beer to order.

MONTROSE

The Twin Cities are two of the most livable big towns in all of North America. But for those who long for small-town existence, there are places such as Montrose, incorporated in 1881, with a population of 1,076. Picturesque homes, a business district offering the essentials, a county historical society— all of this is only about 30 minutes west of Interstate 494 and the west side of Minneapolis. No wonder such villages are becoming bedroom communities.

(For more information, check this Internet site: www.montrosewaverly-chamber.com.)

Bayrischer Hof

631 Nelson Boulevard (Highway 12 West)
Montrose, MN 55363
Telephone: (763) 675-3999
Web site: www.Bayhof.com
Hours: 11 a.m.-2 p.m. Tuesday-Saturday and 4-8:30 p.m. Tuesday-Friday; 3 p.m.-midnight Saturday; 10:30-3 p.m. Sunday.
Nearby attraction: Big and Little Waverly lakes for bass fishing.

Minnesotans and visitors alike always assume there are more descendants of Danes, Finns, Norwegians, or Swedes than any of the other ethnic groups in this farflung state. Fact is, more Germans migrated here than did those from any other country. It is not until the aforementioned Scandinavians are lumped together that they outnumber folks with primarily German ancestors.

Does that explain why a German restaurant is located in Montrose, a small town some 35 miles west of Minneapolis? Travelers who linger a while in Montrose will find that this is a German-American municipality, almost as ethnic as New Ulm, for example. It is no coincidence that Bayrischer Hof, out on Highway 12, replaced a less successful restaurant that was also German.

This is first and foremost a restaurant, with a separate bar operating only on Saturday evenings. Open since 1993, the facility presents customers with eight German tap beers from which to choose: Vorsteiner, Spaten Oktoberfest, Spaten Dunkel, and five kinds of Paulaner. The brews and the food are pungent in the most positive aspects of that word. Who would want anything else?

51

The answer to that question can be found at either lunch or dinner. The No. 1 luncheon item is a bratwurst served with potato salad. The top choice in the evening is a sampler plate bedecked with bratwurst, knockwurst, a smoked pork chop, sauerkraut, and mashed potatoes. There are many other authentic choices, from sauerbraten (marinated beef) to Wiener schnitzel (pan-fried veal). The homemade soups are addictive, sides such as dumpling, noodles, and potato salad are great, and, for those with lots of inner space, there are desserts such as apple strudel and ice cream with hot raspberry sauce.

Fortunately for those who might like to save room in their stomachs for more than one draft, there are several light meals. They provide a diner with smaller servings of the most popular foods. Committed beer drinkers will content themselves with a single smoked pork chop, for example, so that they can sample the variety on tap. A word of warning: German beer goes down easily and can sneak up on a driver. Food helps, but is not a cure-all for excessive imbibing.

Evidently, Germans knew before the rest of us that music goes well with food and refreshment. An accordion player strolls through the dining room Thursday, Friday, and Saturday, and live music may be found in the basement later on most Saturdays. The music downstairs, accompanied by beer, is either authentic German or American polka music with a German accent. It's all good fun, luring regular patrons from places such as St. Cloud, the Twin Cities, and even Hudson, Wisconsin.

Souvenirs and gifts are available here. Besides wines and spirits, there are German candies, hats, cuckoo clocks, figurines, cookbooks, wooden eggs, dolls, nutcrackers, homemade cakes, and more. Ask, too, about the Bayrischer Hof's annual beer fest, held in October. Look for the green-and-white building with the tan brick façade on the north side of Highway 12.

NEW YORK MILLS

Visitors traveling west and exiting four-lane U.S. Highway 10 at New York Mills realize pretty quick that they are in an unconventional small town. To the right at the initial stop sign is a modest but growing sculpture park. An over-size metal gent on an oversize metal tractor provides a pleasant silhouette. Several skinny sculptures done in painted iron may represent either dinosaur bones or Skeezix, one of the bad chaps in *Uncle Wiggly*. There are other artistic efforts, some rather successful.

Unlike many Midwest farm villages, New York Mills is growing. The 2000 census turned up 1,158 residents, an increase from the 943 of a decade earlier. The bump in the population is due to the success of Lund, the local boat manufacturer, Mid-State, an auto auction facility, and several visitors who showed up for the town's biggest annual event, "The Great American Think-Off," and settled in. More about the Think-Off later.

There are dozens of lakes here in Otter Tail Country, most of them west of New York Mills. For those who like the town, there is a career opportunity brewing. In the middle of the pleasant downtown is Glacial Brewery, closed since late 2000. The microbrewery made to-die-for White Tail Ale, but now the place is shuttered and for sale. Locals pledge to support the product of any future brewing entrepreneur.

(For more information, call the Otter Tail Country Tourism Association, (800) 423-4571, or go to their Web site at www.ottertailcountry.com. Or, try the New York Mills *Herald* newspaper web site, www.newyorkmills.com, or the site for the New York Mills Regional Cultural Center, www.kulcher.org.

BEER talk

There are two kinds of malt beverages: those brewed with top-fermenting yeast and those brewed with bottom-fermenting yeast. Virtually all other brews are some sort of variation. With the two major distinctions in mind, here are definitions that should help you choose the kind of beer you might enjoy most.

Ale: A beer made with top-fermenting yeast, fermented at warmer temperatures over a relatively short time. Ales originated in Britain and offer a wide range of colors, aromas, tastes, and strengths.

Altbier: A German-style, top-fermented ale, alt or "old" beer is copper colored, cold-conditioned, and has a flavor similar to a lager.

Bock: Strong beer, usually having more than 6 percent alcohol. Color may be light gold to dark brown. Bocks often are seasonal beers.

Doppelbock: Even stronger, at least 7.5 percent alcohol.

Dunkel: The German word for "dark."

Export: A term used to describe a pale, bottom-fermented beer that is higher in alcohol and has more body than the average pilsner.

Hefe weizen: Literally yeast-wheat, a hefe weizen beer is bottle-conditioned and unfiltered, making for a cloudy appearance.

Kolsch: A top-fermented beer with 4.3 to 5 percent alcohol. The first kolsch beers were made in Cologne.

Lager: This word means "to store," hence beer that is stored so that it can age. Currently, lager is a generic term for bottom-fermented beer. Alcohol levels are 4-5 percent.

Light: This means different things to different people. Americans think of light beer as reduced-calorie (but not necessarily reduced-alcohol) beer, while Europeans think of light as refering to the color of the brew.

Maibock: A pale, high-quality bock beer, usually served at spring (Mai or May) festivals.

Marzen: This medium-strong German beer is made in the month of March; hence the name.

Pale ale: This ale has a crisp hop character and subtle malt richness. Usually it is amber to deep amber in color.

Pilsner: The generic term for bottom-fermented, pale golden lager beer. The term comes from the Czech town of Pilsen, where this widely copied style of beer was developed.

Rauchbier: German for "smoked beer." This is a dark, bottom-fermented beer made from smoked malts in and around Bamberg.

Stout: A dark, strongly flavored (but not necessarily excessively alcoholic) beer.

Weissbier: This is wheat beer, so named for the addition of wheat to the mash. It is a tart and spicy, top-fermented, usually golden beer with relatively low alcohol.

Mills Liquors

26 Centennial 84 Drive
New York Mills, MN 56567
Telephone: (218) 385-2004
Hours: 9 a.m.-midnight Monday-Thursday, 9 a.m.-1 a.m. Friday, Saturday, and holiday eves. Closed major holidays.
Nearby attraction: Finn Creek Museum (restored Finnish farmstead), three miles southeast on Highway 106.

Mills Liquors, to the amazement of visitors, occupies the first floor of the New York Mills City Hall, where it gets prominent billing. It may be one of the very few places on earth where drinkers can do what they do and simultaneously meet the locals, add to the municipal treasury, and feel smug about prices. A bottle of beer here is $1.65, while a 12-ounce tapper is $1.25. Happy hour, 3:30-6 p.m., reduces beer prices by a quarter, and there's always a featured bottle priced at a mere $1.25.

Despite such bargains, "We realize $70,000-$90,000 net profit a year" from Mills Liquors, says City Clerk Wayne Mattson. His office is upstairs, adjacent

Mills Liquors is inside the New York Mills City Hall.

to the 60x90-foot ballroom where wedding receptions and other shindigs take place. Sharing space in the building, which was renovated in 1998, are the fire department and the senior citizens' center. The police are housed several blocks away in the old high school building; Mills Liquors is not the kind of place where the law is needed on a regular basis. In fact, the town has a long and honorable history.

"We opened off-sales during World War II. There had been a bowling alley downstairs since 1939, and in 1959 we began on-sales," Mattson reports. He notes that city ownership allows New York Mills to curb excessive drinking while helping underwrite local government. Besides the American Legion post, the city-owned bar is the only place in town selling "strong beer"—that containing more than 3.2 percent alcohol.

Speaking of which, visitors can expect only megabeers from the four taps. Sandy, the manager, is looking for an on-tap ale to replace Glacial's sorely missed product. Pizza and sandwiches are of the microwave variety, and liquor is available. Visitors happen in to meet each other over a beer, and many brands can be had in bottles. Minnesota stalwarts Schmidt's and Grain Belt join foreign beers that include Beck, Heineken, Molson, and LaBatt in the cooler. The jukebox carries a mix of old and new rock 'n' roll and country-western. Mercifully, karaoke is featured only occasionally, on a weekend evening.

If there is neither music nor conversation, chances are patrons are busy thinking. New York Mills' annual Think-Off poses a philosophical question and names a winner in mid-June on either the pro or con side. An essay from a woman in New York took top honors in 2001. She argued in favor of assisted suicide. Earlier contests have considered questions ranging from whether science or religion is more dangerous to whether man is inherently good or evil. Heavy stuff, covered by CNN and other major media. More information may be found at the New York Mills Regional Cultural Center, 24 Main Avenue North—telephone (218) 385-3339—a handsome brick storefront that houses local and regional art exhibits and keeps regular business hours. Now back to the bar . . .

The interior is cool, contemporary, and inviting. In addition to a dozen or so barstools there are numerous tables with modern, upholstered chairs. Patrons during the day may include farmers who have come to town for errands, retirees, and Twin Cities residents who are here to do some fishing. A booth in the back is staffed by a city employee selling Minnesota's ubiquitous lottery pull-tabs. Mills Liquors is closed Sundays and major holidays.

"We tried to stay open, but everybody went to the lakes," City Clerk Mattson laments. Going to an Otter Tail County lake after stopping in at Mills Liquors seems like a perfect way to prolong a stay.

ST. CLOUD

Said to be Minnesota's fastest-growing city, this municipality on the Mississippi River is known as the source of building stone and as a college town. With 60,076 residents, St. Cloud is about an hour northwest of the Twin Cities via Interstate 94. That's just far enough to maintain its own personality and independence, though a number of locals commute into Minneapolis–St. Paul on a daily basis.

Granite City

3945 Second Street South
St. Cloud, MN 56301
Telephone: (320) 203-9000
Hours: 11 a.m.-1 a.m. (bar); 11 a.m.-midnight (kitchen). Closed Thanksgiving and Christmas.
Nearby attraction: Area fishing and boating lakes.

Should you see a busy fellow in boots scurrying about the newish (since 1999) Granite City brewpub, thank him for crafting the stuff from the tap. He is Bob, an unassuming native of Scotland who holds college degrees in brewing and biology. If the brews here are distinctive—and many people believe them to be—Bob's Scottish training and ability are responsible.

This is a three-story brewing operation, where raw ingredients are delivered to the second floor and fed by gravity through the brewing process to the basement. No kits or other brewing shortcuts are used; the facility cultivates its own yeast, for example. And care is taken to ensure that each beer or ale is served at the proper temperature.

Six different taps are available year round. They include:

• **Northern Light.** As a drinker might suspect, this beer is a low-calorie lager.

• **Victory Lager.** All the calories and flavor a beer drinker expects are available in a Victory.

• **Pride of Pilsen.** Bob puts a Czech spin on his craft, and this is the result.

• **Brother Benedict**. A hearty Maibock will be delivered after uttering the brother's name.

• **Duke of Wellington.** This is an India pale ale, known for its strong and confident flavor.

Granite City, St. Cloud.

- **Broad Axe Stout.** Must a drinker be stout to consume a Broad Axe, or will consumption make a drinker stout? Order up and find out.

There are seasonal beers, too. We enjoyed a raspberry ale and we are given to understand that the Doppelbock, brewed late each year, receives high marks. There are bottled beers, plus wine and liquor. Happy hour runs 4-7 p.m. Monday-Friday.

Spacious, bright, and shiny, Granite City has one of the largest bar areas we ran across, as well as room for many diners. Luncheon favorites include linguini in pesto cream sauce and an Overlake sandwich, which is a turkey BLT grilled and served with aoli mayonnaise. In the evening, lots of diners go for the grilled chicken burrito, while the steak of choice appears to be the London broil.

"This is a destination restaurant," says Al, the manager. "We're known for quality food and huge portions."

Separate lunch and dinner menus afford diners the opportunity to match food and brew to their individual taste. Lighter fare, such as a salad, could be the perfect complement to a glass of Maibock, for example.

The clientele varies with the hour, though the crowd tends to be younger at the bar and a bit older and more family-oriented at the dining tables. College kids have been known to visit, providing they are of age, and beer experts from the Twin Cities stop in on weekends to consume and assess Bob's work. The favorably impressed may buy a hat, a T-shirt, a sweatshirt, or a jacket, or they may visit the two other Granite City locations, in Fargo and Sioux Falls. A disc jockey holds forth a couple of nights a week.

Granite City sits off to the edge of a large shopping center. Second Street South is also Highway 23.

O'Hara's Brew Pub and Restaurant

3308 Third Street North
St. Cloud, MN 56301
Telephone: (320) 251-9877
Hours: 8 a.m.-1 a.m. Monday-Saturday, 10 a.m.-midnight Sunday (bar); 10 a.m.-midnight Monday-Saturday, 10 a.m.-10 p.m. Sunday (kitchen). Closed Christmas.
Nearby attraction: Fifteen area golf courses.

The city of St. Cloud divides itself into downtown, midtown, and west end. O'Hara's is on the line between midtown and the west end, where Third Street and 33rd Avenue intersect. This must be a popular destination; everyone in town seems to know where it is.

Perhaps that is because the brewpub, bar, sports bar, and restaurant combination have all been in business nonstop since 1945. Within the last few years, the folks here have installed a brewing system that offers five crafted beers on tap: honey wheat, red, stout, pale ale, and a seasonal selection. The most popular seasonal beer—raspberry wheat—coincides with the warmest weather. They all taste good.

The kitchen keeps long hours because the food is in demand. The most popular daily lunch specials are hot beef, pork, and turkey sandwiches, with mashed potatoes and a dollop of gravy. Later on, walleye and prime rib vie for top honors, along with a different pasta every evening. The burgers are popular at the bar night and day.

While we admit to an antitelevision bias (it drowns out good bar conversation), there is no question that this is the most popular spot in the city to view a big event. O'Hara's has 27 (count'em!) television sets and seven big-screen TV's placed strategically. It is difficult but not impossible to get away from the blare, and, in defense of the staff, the sets are not running continuously from open to close.

St. Cloud is a popular place for statewide conventions. Consequently, folks from places such as Ely and Warroad and Marshall show up here to hobnob with local people. Many visitors drink a few beers, decide they like the place, and decide to shop for a residence.

Things get lively here on Friday and Saturday nights. A disc jockey spins Top 40 music and dancers spin around the floor. O'Hara's has a full bar, and there are T-shirts and hats adorned with the tavern's iconic, smiling leprechaun. To reach the tavern from I-94, exit east on Highway 23 and turn north onto 33rd Avenue. O'Hara's is five blocks north, on the left. There is parking in a lot behind the facility.

SANDSTONE

The name of this modest village of 2,101, midway between the Twin Cities and Duluth on Interstate 35, strikes fear in the hearts of bad guys everywhere. The town shares its name with the Federal Correctional Institution, where a number of village residents keep an eye on a number of fellows who are under lock and key. More important to the average traveler, Sandstone is as good a place as any to take a break when driving the 150 miles between Minneapolis-St. Paul and Duluth.

For more information, telephone the Sandstone Chamber of Commerce at (320) 245-2271 or check this Web site: www.ci.sandstone.mn.us.

The Gas Light

306 Main St.
Sandstone, MN 55072
Telephone: (320) 245-5344
Hours: 10 a.m.-1 a.m. Monday-Saturday, noon-midnight Sunday. Closed major holidays.
Nearby attraction: Banning State Park, containing the "wild and scenic" Kettle River, is three miles northeast.

The Bonander family learned a few years back that the old Quarrymen's State Bank of Sandstone building was for sale. They acquired the place and turned it into the Gas Light. Before assuming that was an easy or haphazard accomplishment, talk to a family member. They studied books and pulled information and advice off the Internet in preserving some things and restoring others to make having a refreshment an enriching experience.

One look at the bank, in the middle of the downtown area, tells a visitor that the Bonanders have a good eye. The original exterior was preserved, as were the interior's tin walls and tin ceilings. Oak floors were installed for an authentic appearance, and even the lavatory was brought up to date mechanically while retaining the appearance of things that might have been found in a building erected in 1904.

"We tried wherever possible to retain the original look," says Leonard Bonander modestly, adding that the bar opened after renovation was completed in 1999.

There are 50 bottled beers available, from the most modest microbrewery to the most high-powered national. Several foreign brews also are on hand. As this book was going to press, food service was to have begun. For designated drivers, the Gas Light thoughtfully brews fresh espressos and cappuccini. Packaged goods are available for take-out.

History buffs, students of architecture, and those who enjoy traditional beer in a traditional setting will find much to like here. The antique bar was installed after extensive consultation in books such as *America's Historic Inns and Taverns* (by Irvin Haas, the book is now out of print, but available from www.amazon.com). Since this is more or less midway between the Twin Cities and Duluth, drivers headed north or south on Interstate 35 may want to take the well-marked exit (Highway 23 is Main Street) and look for the century-old bank building.

Perhaps some of the inmates housed locally would be shocked and depressed to learn that Quarryman's State Bank has been restored and gone on to better things.

SAUK CENTRE

Sinclair Lewis (1885-1951) was the first American writer to win the international Nobel Prize. Several of his classic novels continue to be assigned in college English classes. The son and grandson of physicians, Lewis was born and reared here. Townspeople at the time were friendly and optimistic, but the author took that as being empty-headed and glad-handing, portraying them as such in *Main Street*.

There was resentment for a while, but having a native son of worldwide repute helped Sauk Centre forgive Lewis for any real or imagined slights. The town, with a current population of 3,866, is small and pleasant, sitting where the woodlands gradually end and the prairie begins. It is yet another Lake Wobegon sort of place, with its own special attractions. There is a scenic bicycle trail, actually named the Lake Wobegon, that runs for approximately twenty miles southeast out of Sauk Centre to Avon. Long and narrow Sauk Lake, just north of town, is especially attractive, said to be filled with fish, and can be seen up close from Highway 71.

(For more information, call (320) 352-5201, or go to the Web at www.saukcentre.com.)

Palmer House

**228 Original Main Street
Sauk Centre, MN 56378
Telephone:** (320) 352-3431
Web site: www.palmerhouse@saukherald.com
Hours: hours vary (bar); 10 a.m.-9 p.m. Mon.-Fri.,
8 a.m.-9 p.m. Sat.-Sun. (kitchen). Closed New Year's Day,
July 4, Thanksgiving, Christmas.
Nearby attraction: Boyhood home of Sinclair Lewis.

Just off the lobby in this century-old hotel is a small bar so evocative of Sinclair Lewis's boyhood era at the turn of the twentieth century that a visitor will swear it is 1908. That was when the famous author worked here as a clerk, chafing at small-town life and no doubt eavesdropping so as to gather material for

Palmer House, Sauk Centre.

his books. Lewis went on to win the Nobel Prize, in 1930, and to write such still-read bestsellers as *Main Street, Babbitt, Arrowsmith, Elmer Gantry,* and *Dodsworth.*

The bar has a beige-painted tin ceiling and green walls. The fixtures, the furniture, and the bar itself speak of a time when salespeople gathered after a long day of calling on customers, or when retailers stopped here after tallying up the day's receipts.

Perhaps the easiest way to pass some time in the bar is to stay overnight. Owners Stan and Cathy Schmidt offer sixteen rooms and suites (priced admirably at $39-$99) in an atmospheric three-story brick building that also houses a popular restaurant. Folks who work along what is now named Original Main Street come here for the luncheon buffet, which features different dishes every day. In the evening, locals and guests break bread over entrees such as prime rib.

Cathy made a wrong turn and ended up in Sauk Centre a few years back. A chef in New York State and an auctioneer, she bought a Sauk Centre Victorian home to restore, then purchased the hotel. Cathy says the hotel and restaurant are especially popular with cyclists, who come here from the Twin Cities for the Lake Wobegon trail ride. The Sinclair Lewis salute in mid-July each year also packs the house, and birders have been known to stay over, binoculars and notebooks in hand.

SOUTHERN
Minnesota

ONCE the Mississippi joins the St. Croix to form Minnesota's southeastern border, it really begins to look like America's biggest river. There are stretches of the river valley between Minnesota and Wisconsin that are several miles wide. Drive Highway 61 either north or south and you will be on one of Bob Dylan's favorite routes, as well as one of the most scenic roads in the entire country.

From here west, travelers pass imposing bluffs that make a quick transition into rich farmland separated by occasional towns and patches of woods that diminish as you travel west. The woods are quite thin in the southwest, there are ecologically important potholes and wetlands, and all of the land here is fertile. Summer's long days favor the growth of corn, beans, and any variety of wheat.

Southern Minnesota was settled as early as the Civil War, with the Minnesota River valley offering abundant land to Germans and other European settlers. Native Americans last put up a fight here in 1862, killing a number of first-generation settlers and setting newly built villages alight. A few years later, the Twin Cities became a huge grain hub, thanks in part to the agricultural productivity of this region.

Today, many visitors whistle north or south on Interstate 35, or east or west on Interstate 90, oblivious to the charms just beyond any off-ramp. Lakes are ubiquitous between Faribault and Mankato, and common elsewhere. Every town of any size has someone famous with roots here, whether it be former football coach and TV commentator John Madden, the late rocker Eddie Cochran, or author Laura Ingalls Wilder. Consider stopping awhile, swimming or fishing, and meeting tomorrow's sports star, rocker, or rural intellectual.

ELBA

There are several good reasons for visiting tiny Elba, population 231, about a dozen miles northwest of Winona in the Whitewater Valley. First, if travelers enjoy the bluffs that line the Mississippi River, they will appreciate the bluffs that serve as backdrop here. Rugged countryside interspersed with rich farm-land makes for a most attractive area.

Hardwood, hunting, and Harley-Davidsons appear to be the big attractions. The main street is Highway 74, which intersects with Highway 248 in Elba.

Jonny's Saloon

Highway 74
Elba, MN 55910
Telephone: (507) 932-4969
Hours: 8 a.m.-1 a.m., Monday-Saturday,
10 a.m.-1 a.m. Sunday.
Nearby attraction: Elba Fire Tower National Historic Lookout.

What would it take to get you inside a biker bar? A cordial host? Friendly customers? Craft-brewed beer? How about two out of three? Jonny's Saloon is the only tavern in this book where a visitor will find lots of motorcycles parked out front. And while the tap beer isn't very imaginative, the help is nice and the drinkers don't mind strangers.

Jonny's is next to a motorcycle repair shop. The bikers' machines glisten in an orderly row and the owners of these V-twins are gotten up in vests, gloves, bandanas, T-shirts, boots, and such. They have taken to drinking inside and out, weather permitting, and nobody seems to mind.

Inside, the only tap beer available is Michelob. The stalk-like handle awaits the next pull. There are several beers in bottles, though in truth the only re-motely exotic brew may well be Corona. Jonny has been in business since 1978, so either his customers are content with the few beers he offers, or they opt for one of his liquor concoctions.

We motored (on four wheels) into Jonny's on a Sunday afternoon in the late fall. The jukebox was pumpin', there was a NASCAR race on one TV set and Vikings football on another, folks were shooting pool, tossing darts, and playing one of several video games. Surprisingly for the motorcycle crowd,

Jonny's Saloon, Elba.

there is a video golf game that gets some attention. The crowd was a mix of bikers, hunters, fishers, and other locals, though not many tourists. Visitors who are also bike riders show up regularly in warm weather.

"This is a saloon, not a grill," Jonny reminds us. Therefore, he offers pizza, sandwiches, and wings, but no burgers or fries. Patrons who are hungry must have learned to dine before hopping off their bikes here. Which reminds us— it appeared that American-made machines were parked at the near curb and Japanese bikes across the street. We could be wrong, but there may well be a vehicular code of conduct.

Happily, there is no specific way to behave at Jonny's, inside or out, though returning a smile is as good a way to introduce yourself as any. It also doesn't hurt to wear a black T-shirt, jeans, and chaps. Regardless, the saloon adheres to Jonny's motto, which is, "A friendly place where friends meet."

FARIBAULT

Nearly 20,000 people call this place home, where the Cannon and Straight rivers meet. It is an attractive and industrious place, and one can only imagine what it must have been like when Alexander Faribault came here in 1826 to trap fur. Faribault built a home that still stands; it is open for tours.

The town evolved into a most humane burg, serving as the home for education of the state's hearing-impaired and the state's sight-impaired. It has a number of pleasant surprises, from lakes rimmed by resorts to a direct link of only about 50 miles via Interstate 35 to the Twin Cities. Among several annual events, two local festivals are set for the same mild weekend in mid-September: a balloon rally and a music festival. It should be noted that the latter includes a beer garden.

For a glimpse at what the area was like before Europeans arrived, head to Nerstrand Big Woods State Park, 10 miles northeast of town. This 1,300-acre park has more than a dozen miles of hiking trails. They wind among elms, maples, and other huge trees that soar 100 feet or more into the blue. Back in town, contact the Faribault Area Convention and Tourism office at (800) 658-2354 or (507) 334-4381, or go to their Web site at www.faribaultmn.org.

The Depot Bar and Grill

311 Heritage Place
Faribault, MN 55021
Telephone: (507) 332-2825
Hours: 11 a.m.-1 a.m. (bar); 11 a.m.-midnight (kitchen). Closed major holidays.
Nearby attraction: River Bend Nature Center hiking trails.

Every Minnesota town with a museum or historical society has old photos of when the railroads were big. Lean, tough men pose with picks and shovels along rails of steel that opened up this part of the continent. Faribault was served, at one time or another, by the Chicago Great Western, the Minnesota and Northwestern, the Chicago, St. Paul and Kansas, the Milwaukee Road, the

The Depot Bar and Grill, Faribault.

Burlington Road, and the Rock Island Line. With the demise of rail travel, other uses had to be made of depots. This is a worthwhile use.

The same family has owned the Depot since it opened in 1992. Perhaps that is why the food is fresh and care has been given to the refreshments. Tap beers include the familiar nationals: Budweiser, Miller Golden Draft, Michelob Golden Draft, Miller Lite, Summit Extra Pale Ale, three kinds of Leinenkugel's, and LaBatt's. In short, something for virtually every taste. Several additional brands are available by the bottle, and there is full wine and liquor service.

Homemade soup meets homemade bread in a soup-and-sandwich special at lunch every day. Other in-demand noonday items include a gyro sandwich, a chicken sandwich, a hot beef sandwich, and several pasta plates. For dinner, steaks and seafood head the list, and there are pasta choices and a full complement of appetizers, salads, side dishes, and desserts. A late-night menu kicks in at 10 p.m. Happy hour, which offers half-price beer, runs 3:30-6 p.m. For those who consider their stop here memorable there are hats and T-shirts. The classic rock piped into the facility is not overpowering.

In warm weather, look for a place to drink and dine outside. The help is young and helpful, while the clientele includes a nice range of ages, from a fellow who just turned 21 to a couple well into their retirement years.

The Depot is a bit out of the way but worth finding. From Interstate 35, exit southeast onto Highway 21 (Lyndale Avenue). Turn left or east onto Fourth Street and continue through town east to Heritage Place. The restaurant, with the railroad and the Straight River behind it, should be visible at that point.

LAKE CITY

Like a number of Minnesota villages, Lake City harbors a few surprises. Pulling into town, travelers discover that this is the birthplace of water skiing. Seems a local resident sized up his snow skis, assessed the speed of Chris-Crafts racing back and forth on the Mississippi, and realized he could have himself pulled along on the surface of the big river.

At this point on the Mississippi, the water actually is known as Lake Pepin. The lake is where the river widens to accommodate such things as the mouth of Wisconsin's Chippewa River. In something of a bowl, the wide, bluff-rimmed area can be treacherous as winds howl up and down it. But it is undeniably great for sailing, which is why there is a large, well-stocked marina on the south side of town.

For additional information, call the Wabasha Area Chamber of Commerce at (800) 565-4158, or (651) 565-4158, or check the Web site at www.wabashamn.org.

Waterman's

1702 Lakeshore Drive (Highway 61)
Lake City, MN 55041
Telephone: (651) 345-5353
Hours: 11 a.m.-11 p.m. (bar); 11 a.m.-10 p.m. (kitchen).
Closed Thanksgiving, Christmas.
Nearby attraction: Lake Pepin (the Mississippi River).

Nickey, who manages Waterman's, has a problem. The exterior of this bar and restaurant is handsome to the point that folks sometimes feel that they may be underdressed and so go somewhere else.

"We're a casual place!" she says, adding that the new, 60-ft. deck is a great summertime spot to relax with a cool drink as the river flows inexorably south. With Lake Pepin in the side yard, why look at anything else?

Five beers are on tap here and may be enjoyed outside or in the bar or restaurant, which are separate. Look for Leinenkugel, Bud Light, Guinness, Harp, and Michelob Amber Bock. Additional brands are available by the bottle, and there are wines by the glass and by the bottle, as well as mixed drinks.

Waterman's, Lake City.

The restaurant offers a full menu. Attractive luncheon items include fish or Reuben sandwiches, both of which Nickey says people return to consume. A special fish dinner is offered Friday nights, and there are prime rib specials Friday and Saturday evenings. Other entrees for which customers clamor include Cajun chicken fettucine and walleye.

Happily for nonsmokers, there is a porch on which to drink or dine. Entertainment is booked only occasionally, probably because the view is entertainment enough.

On the east side of Highway 61 and on the north side of town, Waterman's is part of the Willows condominium complex. There are many restaurants, resorts, and taverns in Minnesota situated on the water, but none are superior to this sweeping view. On a July weekend afternoon, with sailboats, powerboats, and barges moving up and down, the vista across to Wisconsin is among the most picturesque in the entire country.

MANKATO

This is where the Minnesota and Blue Earth rivers meet, amid several impressive prominences. The city of 32,355, along with North Mankato (population 11,844), has been constructed up, down, and all around. Much of downtown Mankato is low-lying, whereas Mankato State University's 13,000 students find themselves high up on a table of land that is reached by a lengthy climb from the business district. Mankato and North Mankato are separated by the Minnesota River. Leafy Land of Memories Park, west of downtown, is the spot where the rivers converge.

The Indians must have been quite impressed with the immediate area. The land around the two rivers is an ancient Dakota burial site. Each year in September, Native Americans come from all over to participate in the Mahkato (which means Blue Earth) Mdewakaton Pow Wow. The Dakota conflict ended in 1862, during the Civil War. It is to the settlers' everlasting shame that Indians were hanged here in the largest mass execution ever conducted on U.S. soil.

On a brighter note, the area today serves as a shopping center for south-central Minnesota. Increasingly, the people who run things realize that this is an attractive city. Much of it is visible from biking and hiking paths, which have been greatly expanded in the last few years.

(For additional information, call the Mankato Area Chamber and Convention Bureau at 800/657-4733, or 507-345-4519, or check this Web site: www.mankato.com.)

McGoff's Irish Pub & Eatery

113 E. Hickory St.
Mankato, MN 56001
Telephone: (507) 387-4000
Hours: 11 a.m.-1 a.m. Mon.-Fri..; 10 a.m.-1 a.m.
Sat.-Sun. Closed Easter Sunday, Memorial Day,
Thanksgiving, Christmas.
Nearby attraction: Several long and interesting biking and
hiking trails.

Where *would* we be without the Irish? Those guys built most of the rail-roads, at least as far west as Utah. Equally crucial, had there been no potato famine in the 19th century, such fine establishments as McGoff's might not exist. That would be unfortunate, since this small and unassuming tavern does a couple of things better than virtually anyone else in the state.

First, it offers a 20-oz. glass of Weihenstephan for just $2.75. This rare German beer is from what is billed as the world's oldest brewery (established 1040 A.D.). Second, McGoff's remembers its heritage by organizing a tour of Ireland each October. In addition to nine days and eight nights of visiting Irish pubs, the lads and lasses receive a tour of the Guinness brewery and a similar visit to Murphy's, another famous brewer of stout. Would that more taverns were so attentive to and cognizant of their roots!

McGoff's is in the shadow of the Mankato Civic Center, one block south of the Mankato Place parking ramp. There are 15 taps, pouring brews from the prosaic to such sublime drafts as Bass Ale, Guinness, Harp, Murphy's, and others. The quality and quantity of beer and ale available by the bottle is, well, staggering—seventy different labels are offered. Liquor is available, but it is of less consequence to the vast majority of visitors.

Customers are an interesting collection, including the downtown lunch crowd, a few retirees, some college kids, an out-of-town shopper or two, a couple of beer savants, and even the occasional vacationer. All of them appreciate a happy hour that begins at 3 p.m. and runs for three hours Monday-Friday. They appreciate the food, too.

Lunch might be an authentic shepherd's pie, or one of several sandwiches or wraps. Dinner is more sumptuous, with favorites including prime rib, salmon, walleye, and a Guinness-flavored beef stew. After dinner on Fridays and Saturdays, folks gather to hear whatever Irish band happens to have been booked. Music at other times is digital and could be Irish, light rock, or blues. Warm weather features patio dining, and there are T-shirts and hats to commemorate a visit.

Asked what he would most like visitors to know, John, the manager, said, "That we're the best tavern in southern Minnesota."

MANTORVILLE

Little more than a crossroads northwest of Rochester, Mantorville serves as a hometown for a number of people employed in the complex of medical facilities in Rochester. Those folks may have moved here in part to enjoy views of several architecturally significant old buildings. They vary, from the remains of Mantorville's first brewery (1858) to the Dodge County Courthouse (1871). Visitors should turn north off Highway 14 onto Highway 57 and travel through Kasson to reach this destination.

The Mantorville Chamber of Commerce offers a free map of the village and its 19th- and early 20th-century structures. For more information, call Riverside Gifts, (507) 635-5464, or check this Web site: www.Mantorville.com.

Hubbell House

Highway 57 (Main Street)
Mantorville, MN 55955
Telephone: (507) 635-2331
Web site: www.hubbell-house.com
Hours: 11:30 a.m.-2 p.m., 5 p.m.-close, Tuesday-Saturday; 11:30 a.m.-close Sundays. Closed most holidays.
Nearby attraction: Mantorville Theatre (acting troupe).

How's this for a good deal? Travelers who stop at Hubbell House in tiny (population 1,029) Mantorville can avail themselves of fine dining in a Civil War–era atmosphere while they sample what could be the rarest microbrewed ale in the state.

Hubbell House, a couple of miles north of Highway 14, which runs between Rochester and Owatonna, has been attending to visitors since it opened in 1854 as a stagecoach stop and hotel. With a dining room and a bar evocative of days gone by, the cream-colored limestone building is faithfully patronized by folks from Rochester and elsewhere in southeastern Minnesota.

Diners who spend time in the bar can order Mantorville Stage Coach Ale, a full-bodied drink made literally around the corner by the Mantorville Brewing Company. This tiny enterprise, in a building perhaps the size of a multi-car garage, is where a fellow from the Twin Cities and a couple of local guys spend their weekends brewing two different beers. Other than sharing the same small town, the only connection between Hubbell House and the microbrewery is the bar's desire to serve—and the brewery's desire to craft—good beer.

The beer must be good; it sells as well as any of the several other taps available. They include Budweiser, Michelob Golden Light, Michelob Draft, Leinenkugel Red, and Leinenkugel Honey Weiss. The bar also serves liquor, but it would be a shame to drink anything else when there are so few outlets for Mantorville Stage Coach Ale.

The brew also is a worthwhile accompaniment to the food. Don, the owner and manager, is part of a family that has been serving guests here since 1946. He notes that there are separate lunch and dinner menus and that popular luncheon entrees include barbecue ribs and homemade, beer-battered chicken strips.

Favored main courses in the evening are filet mignon and jumbo shrimp. Walleye is available beer-battered or broiled, and occasionally pan-seared. Side dishes are fresh and cleverly prepared, and there are some great desserts—Hubbell Turtle Pie, bread pudding, and crème brulee come immediately to mind.

Mother's Day is the restaurant's busiest day each year. Dare we ask you to buy your mom a Mantorville Stage Coach Ale at Hubbell House? Indeed! Where else will she find something interesting to drink that is carefully concocted just east of the fire hall by quality-oriented fellows devoted to beer? Now that we think about it, why wait for Mother's Day?

NEW ULM

New Ulm traces its roots back to 19th-century Bohemia, a state in what is now Germany. Revolutions tore through Europe in 1848, kicking off an out-migration that did not end until the eve of World War I. The site for New Ulm, in the rich Minnesota River valley, was chosen in 1854. Three years later, the Turner Colonization Society of Cincinnati and the Chicago Land Society, both made up of German-Americans, merged and incorporated the town. Steamboats carrying troops to fight the Indians sailed past here, and the town was overrun and set afire by Indians in 1862. Through the years, the area also survived an infestation of grasshoppers and a cyclone. Residents have always realized the importance of their U.S. and German heritage, both of which are evident everywhere from the telephone book to the tavern.

Tune the radio dial to KNUJ at 860 on the AM dial. Chances are, polka, that joyous blast of tavern music with origins in Central Europe, will set toes tapping. Glide past the Minnesota Music Hall of Fame, where local stars such as the Almost Sisters and Schell's Hobo Band are enshrined. Above all, check out Broadway in the downtown area, for virtual wall-to-wall retail with a Bohemian touch. The town's older residential areas, including several restored homes, are dotted with striking architecture, most of it devoid of the kitschy stuff applied to the downtown storefronts.

(For more information, call the Visitor Information Center at (888) 463-9856 or (507) 233-4300, or visit this Web site: www.newulm.com.)

THE ULTIMATE
beer food

Lots of eats go well with beer: Pizza in front of TV, a car battery–size piece of cheese in front of TV, a bologna the length of a baseball bat in front of TV. There is one product, however, that is so well attuned to beer that it may be eaten with great satisfaction even when there is nothing worth watching on television. That product is Spam.

Slightly salty, ready for any condiment, enhancer, slice of cheese or hunk of bread the consumer cares to add, Spam has been in American pantries since 1937. Generations come and go, but the number of Spam fans seems to be perpetual. Thank heavens Hormel Foods opened a museum devoted to the apparent meat product in 2001.

Hormel has, since 1881, been offering meats out of its home in Austin, Minnesota. While the company makes other well-known products—Dinty Moore beef stew, Dubuque Plumpers hot dogs—they are best known for the compact, rectangular, blue-and-yellow can and its contents.

The edible is so ubiquitous locally that Austin goes by the nickname Spamtown. The women's chorus calls itself the Spamettes. Folks here have grown up on Spam and other Hormel products, and they certainly look none the worse for wear. The 16,5550-square-foot museum, an "old market" design, offers kiosks, videos, samples of Spamburgers and Spam luncheon meat specialties, plus Spam souvenirs.

Just off Interstate 90 and less than 20 miles east of Interstate 35, the museum is at 1937 Spam Boulevard. Hours are 10 a.m.-5 p.m. Monday-Saturday and noon-4 p.m. Sunday. The telephone number is (800) LUVSPAM. Like bar hors d'oeuvres served during happy hour, admission is free. For more information, click on Spam Museum when you visit http://www.spam.com.

August Schell Brewing Company

18th Street South, west of Broadway
New Ulm, MN 56073
Telephone: (507) 354-5528
Web site: www.schellsbrewery.com
Hours: Tours are at 3 and 4 p.m. Wednesday and 1, 2, 3, and 4 p.m. Saturday and Sunday, Memorial Day–Labor Day; tours are at 1 and 2:30 p.m. Saturday, Nov.-May.
Nearby attraction: The parklands surrounding the brewery.

If there were no August Schell Brewing Company, someone would have to invent it. The brewery, the Schell home, and the grounds, west of Broadway (State Route 15) in this most German of all Minnesota towns, is a quaint, attractive place. More important for those who enjoy beer, the facility produces 13 different brews totaling almost 60,000 barrels annually. Schell products are available in Minnesota and parts of North and South Dakota, Iowa, Wisconsin, Illinois, Michigan, Ohio, and Pennsylvania.

This second-oldest family-owned and managed U.S. brewery came to life in 1858 with the arrival of August Schell. Two years later he rolled his first beer barrel onto the delivery wagon. New Ulm burned during the Dakota Conflict of 1862, but because the brewers got along with the local Indians, the enterprise was spared. By 1880 the beer was the region's largest seller, and five years after that, the Schells constructed a mansion, flower garden, and deer park. But for Prohibition, when near-beer and soda were offered, the brewery has produced a variety of beers and ales ever since.

And what variety! With its tours, Schell hands out a flyer that lists the following products: Pils, a pilsener made with 100 percent barley malt and a mix of imported and domestic hops; Firebrick Lager, an all-malt Vienna-style lager; German Pale Ale, an amber ale with pronounced bitterness and marked aroma; Schmalt'z Ale, a very dark double ale; Doppel Bock, a dark beer with amber highlights; Maifest, a blonde bock; Zommerfest, an effervescent, golden ale; Octoberfest, a reddish-caramel ale with four kinds of hops; Snow Storm Beer, a 100 percent malt product; Bock, with a straw color and Schell's own yeast; Original, an American lager; and Light, a low-calorie beer. Root beer, dubbed 1919, is also brewed, and is available only on draft.

All of the beers and ales are either specialty, specialty/seasonal, premium, or super-premium. They are available at virtually every tavern in town and at very good prices. Stores carry a variety of Schell in bottles.

Schell Brewing Company grounds, New Ulm.

Besides the brewery, guests can spend time in the museum, the gift house, and on the scenic grounds. (The mansion is not open to the public.) Schell charges two dollars for the tour and sampling afterward. The gift shop and museum are open every day noon-5 p.m. Memorial Day–Labor Day and the shop is open noon-5 p.m. Saturday and Sunday the rest of the year. Travelers who find themselves in New Ulm in February will want to attend Bock Fest, which is held in and around the brewery. The event is publicized as a chance to drive winter away early and is held the same day as Fasching, the traditional German pre-Lent celebration.

This is not a place the ordinary traveler is apt to run across. Look for the signs pointing west off Broadway, then take the first left after driving onto 18th Street South. The road winds through a park and dead-ends at the brewery. The side trip is worth it.

Turner Hall

102 S. State St.
New Ulm, MN 56073
Telephone: (507) 354-4916
Hours: 8 a.m.-closing. Closed Easter and Christmas.
Nearby attraction: The Hermann Monument, erected in 1897.

A sense of history meets great beer prices inside Turner Hall, where the Club Room or rathskeller awaits, down half a flight of stairs. The tavern inside this National Register of Historic Places structure displays restored, ancient murals of an idyllic Europe, probably painted by a German-American yearning for the fatherland. Both immigrants and residents of long standing will enjoy this place, constructed of imposing red brick in 1872.

A plaque out front tells visitors that "The Turner concept of developing a sound mind and body through discussion of common problems and physical exercise was conceived by Frederick Turner of Berlin in 1811. It was an effort to strengthen German resolve against the French conqueror, Napoleon." The result is that hundreds of children take gymnastics classes in the facility, though the folks at the bar and at tables in the Club Room don't seem to have any problems worth airing. The facility is supported by seven hundred members, paying $50 annually, and by rental of the gymnasium and dining room for weddings, reunions, etc.

Three taps grace the bar, which is open to the general public. They dispense Schell Original, Schell Light, and Miller Golden Draft. A 12-oz. draft is $1.25, while a similar-sized bottle is $2; these prices beat most other taverns' happy hours. Speaking of happy, the fellows around the U-shaped bar during out visit looked tranquil, though none of them went upstairs to practice their somersaults. Liquor is available in quite some variety, and there is a sound system that plays polkas and other music, but no jukebox.

Ask the bartender to point out the Dutch Room, a place where proper ladies waited years ago so that their men could stay in the bar, drinking and smoking cigars. If a traveler is fortunate, the barkeep will be Elmer Scheid, head of a seven-piece polka band that has played far and wide. Though Elmer is eighty years of age, he and his band still entertain at an occasional Oktoberfest or other ethnic get-together. Elmer is of course enshrined in the nearby Minnesota Music Hall of Fame.

Speaking of tunes, Friday nights are the times to catch a local or regional German musical group here. The entertainment is so authentic that a group of Germans a few years back visited and were all but swept away by music no longer heard all that frequently in their homeland. German-Americans, it ap-

Turner Hall, New Ulm.

pears, have done a better job than most of keeping tradition alive down through the years.

Music, brews, and conviviality can make a person hungry, and food is available whenever the bar is open. Lunches include chicken, shrimp, and burgers, together with onion rings and an array of appetizers. Rich Runck, who manages the entire hall, has been known to prepare meals while he juggles two or three other pressing matters.

The longer travelers linger here, the more they are likely to learn. This building once housed a German high school, called at the time an academy. That did not stop rathskeller activity, and neither did Prohibition. Moonshine in particular was purchased from stills along the Minnesota River and covertly consumed. There is nothing covert about Turner Hall or the Club Room these days. It is a most popular step back into America as it once was.

RED WING

This stretch of the Mississippi River has been called the Hiawatha Valley, perhaps because Henry Wadsworth Longfellow's poem was popular at about the time the first Europeans settled here. A number of them, approximately 900, were off-loaded by steamboats in 1857. They must have been skilled potters, because Red Wing quickly became known for the production of dishes, bowls, crocks, and jugs.

The first train to arrive here followed the river north, easing into town in 1871. The railroads put the steamboats out of business, but today a visitor can, from a relaxing bench on the levee, watch a number of barges move coal, grain, gravel, and other material up and down the Mississippi. By 1940, there was a city-owned airport, but it was in a rather unusual spot. Wisconsin must have had fewer bluffs and coulees, because, to this day, the Red Wing facility is across the river in Bay City.

With the pottery business long gone, but with some 4,000 collectors of Red Wing pottery showing up every summer, this town of 15,883 is a handsome place in a handsome setting. For more information, telephone (800) 498-3444 or (651) 385-5934. To view matters on the Web, go to www.redwing.org.

Jimmy's Bar (in the St. James Hotel)

406 Main Street
Red Wing, MN 55066
Telephone: (651) 388-2846
Hours: 4 p.m.-1 a.m. Monday-Saturday, 1 p.m.-1 a.m. Sunday.
Nearby attraction: The Mississippi River.

Jimmy's is a nice spot in the evocative, old, immaculate St. James Hotel, exactly the kind of tavern travelers would hope to find, whether or not they are staying the night in one of the hotel's sumptuously decorated rooms.

Before the architecture or the décor turns our heads, let's head for the beer taps. Jimmy's pledges to change beers with the seasons; when we were there, we found Schell wheat beer, plus Guinness, Bass Ale, Summit, and Schell products. There are bottled beers just out of sight, and wine and liquor are poured here, too.

St. James Hotel, home of Jimmy's Bar, Red Wing.

Craig, the hotel manager, notes that the bar is actually a reproduction of a British pub. Perhaps that is why so many Black-and-Tan orders, made authentically with Bass and Guinness, are taken here. The stained glass and the rich, dark woodwork are the perfect counterpoint to the glare off river water on a sunny day. Cigars are available, as are a number of hand-crafted bourbons and single-malt scotches. Because the place is well ventilated, nonsmokers should have no problems.

Perhaps the hotel is best known for a recent *Wine Spectator* magazine award, which in truth was handed to the Port, the hotel's upscale, dinner-only restaurant. For wine lovers, there are several estimable vintages at the bar. In turn, a beer can be had while dining at the Port or at the Veranda, which serves breakfast, lunch, and dinner. As a visitor might suspect, the Veranda offers alfresco food and drink in warm weather.

Quality entertainment is sometimes hard to find in a modest-sized town, but it is not a problem here. Friday nights, a female cabaret singer holds forth inside Jimmy's. She is the most frequently booked talent, but there also is a jazz combo that performs here from time to time. Should a drinker develop more hunger than thirst, pub foods such as burgers and an array of appetizers may be ordered. Move to either restaurant for a complete meal.

The four-story St. James is Red Wing's most attractive building. It is the centerpiece of tourism efforts and an enviable visitor destination between Chicago and the Twin Cities. It is also less than an hour from Minneapolis or St. Paul, which means that a fair number of metro residents come here for dining or lodging.

ROCHESTER

A sharp-eyed visitor to this medically focused city will notice circular, blue-and-green medallions affixed to some of the local storm sewers. The emblems warn against dumping any toxic substance, because "it will end up in the lake." Ironically, there is no lake in this city of 82,019, Minnesota's fourth largest. Surrounding Olmsted County also is lake-free—the only county in the state without its own natural fishin' and swimmin' hole. Nevertheless, the Zumbro River has been dammed north of Rochester, producing a body of water suitable for all sorts of aquatic recreation.

The not-quite lake isn't the only anomaly. Rochester's downtown would do justice to a city two or three times its size. The area houses many of the Mayo Clinic's forty-seven structures, including such biggies as the new, 24-story Gonda Building. The diagnostic skills of the world's largest private medical center are why such luminaries as the late King of Jordan and former Beatle George Harrison fly quietly into the airport south of town. One result of the number of skilled medical jobs is that there are allegedly eleven single women for every single man here.

Rochester has a reputation as a family town. *Money* magazine consistently rates it one of the best places to live in America. (For more information, dial the Rochester Convention and Visitors Bureau at (800) 634-8277 or (507) 288-4331, or visit this Web site: www.rochestercvb.org.)

Broadstreet Café and Bar/Redwood Room

300 First Ave. N. W.
Rochester, MN 55901
Telephone: (507) 281-2451
Web site: www.broastreet-café.com
Hours: 11 a.m.-9:30 p.m. Monday-Friday, 5 p.m.-9:30 p.m.
Saturday-Sunday (Café); 11 a.m.-2 p.m. Monday-Friday;
4:30-11 p.m. Monday-Thursday, 4:30 p.m.-midnight
Friday-Saturday, 4:30-10 p.m. Sunday (Redwood Room).
Closed major holidays.
Nearby attraction: Twenty-nine miles of city bicycle trails.

About the time travelers despair of ever finding a great place for a drink in Rochester, they discover these two spots, one on top of the other. The café, on the ground floor, serves good food along with its refreshments, while the basement Redwood Room offers live jazz or blues every evening, without so much as a cover charge. They share a picturesque brick building at First Avenue and Civic Center Drive, alongside the railroad track.

The café has half a dozen stools at its bar and a dazzling, mirrored back bar. The entire place is shiny, spotless, and upscale, while the venue below is darker and more conducive to beer drinking and tale telling. No tap beers are served up top, but visitors can choose from such exotic bottled beers and ales as "Old Speckled Hen" English Ale or Czechoslovakia's famed Pilsener Urquell. The wine list has to be among the most extensive anywhere outside of the Twin Cities metro area. The Redwood Room has at least twice as many barstools and such tap treats as Guinness, Hacker Pschorr, and Leinenkugel Red. Perhaps because this is a health-conscious city, both restaurants are smoke-free.

Food favorites upstairs include cream chicken enchiladas, seafood garlic pasta, and walleyed pike at lunch, and stuffed chicken breast, pecan-crusted venison, grilled elk chop, and grilled duck breast at dinner. The menu one floor below offers everything from gourmet pizzas, with toppings such as grilled duck or gorgonzola cheese, to entrees such as mixed grill or filet of salmon. Despite the fact that people from all over the world show up in Rochester to be examined and treated, the crowd here is predominantly local. In warm weather they spill out onto the deck, on the same side of the building as the smallish parking lot.

The patrons share the opinion that music makes a drink go down easy, so when the tunes start (as early as 6:30 p.m. weekdays and 7 p.m. weekends), they frequently head downstairs at the end of a meal. They also may linger up-

91

Broadstreet Café and Bar/Redwood Room, Rochester.

stairs for dessert, which features decadence such as chocolate lava cake or caramel nut tartlet. Save room for beer.

Taverns closer to the Mayo Clinic, or to either of the city's two hospitals, are sometimes filled with patients, or families of patients, with a lot on their minds. So if a vacationer is feeling carefree and wants to maintain that feeling, these spots may be the best destinations in town.

ST. PETER

St. Peter, Minnesota, is an idyllic town (pop. 10,038) approximately 70 miles southwest of the Twin Cities. Situated on U.S. Hwy. 169, it is known throughout Minnesota as a progressive place and a center for the arts. An initial drive through this clean and well-preserved town turns up many restored buildings, Gustavus Adolphus College on a west-side hill, and the Minnesota River flowing by.

The town also is the seat of Nicollet County. West of town is Swan Lake, the largest shallow-prairie pothole in North America. East a few miles, in neighboring LeSueur County, there are a number of smaller lakes. The Treaty Site History Center museum, which fetes an 1851 Indian treaty, is just to the north on Hwy. 169, while a major attraction in town is the St. Peter Regional Treatment Center. This still-active institution was the first psychiatric treatment facility in the state (1866). There is no known connection between the treatment center and the fact that five governors have called St. Peter home.

(For more information, call the St. Peter Tourism and Visitors Bureau at (800) 473-3404, or (507) 934-3400, or check this Web site: www.tourism.st-peter.mn.us.)

A typically well-preserved storefront, downtown St. Peter.

Patrick's

125 S. Third St.
St. Peter, MN 56082
Telephone: (507) 931-9051
Hours: 11 a.m.-1 a.m. (bar); 11 a.m.-midnight (kitchen).
Closed Christmas Day.
Nearby attraction: Numerous downtown buildings on the
National Register of Historic Places.

That thing atop Patrick's, the Irish-German bar and grill in downtown St.
Peter, is a horn. Specifically, it is a contra bass, a tuba-type instrument, and it
symbolizes that Patrick's is the headquarters of the Governaires, the oldest
competing drum and bugle corps on earth. On any given day, look for a green
school bus in front of the tavern. That's transportation for the corps, which
performs all over. John, the bar owner's son, works at the bar, manages the en-
semble, and plays percussion.

Patrick's, St. Peter.

With a built-in band of drinkers (the drummers, the buglers), is there room for a stranger at the bar? Indeed there is, and the good news here is that there are sixteen taps offering a most pleasing array of brews. Three kinds of Schell are backed up by Guinness, two kinds of Summit, Harp, Honker's Ale, 1919 Draft Root Beer, and more. Should there be nothing that pleases from the taps, there are numerous bottled brews available, including Corona and other Mexican beers.

Mexican food is served for lunch Monday-Friday and as late as 9 p.m. on Fridays only. Look for the usual: burritos, chimichangas, enchiladas, nachos, quesadillas, and tacos, from mild to fiery. The evening menu is more expansive. In addition to chicken, rib, and either rib eye or T-bone dinners, there are appetizers, sandwiches, soups, salads, burgers, wraps, and chicken, fish, shrimp, or drummie baskets. The signature sandwich is a patty melt, and pizzas with the usual toppings are readily available.

Patrick's is in a spacious brick building, one of many in the downtown area that are both old and in good condition. The town is fortunate that the venerable buildings are still standing, since a tornado ripped through here in 1998, killing one person and doing a lot of damage. The tavern has a lengthy bar and a couple of rooms for dining and drinking. A Touchtunes computer with 750 songs provides a lively touch. Several new songs are downloaded every evening and may be anything from Metallica to Sinatra. It is even possible to phone in a request!

Like migrant labor, the crowd here is seasonal. The bar is absolutely overrun on Gustavus Adolphus College football Saturdays, and there are a number of chamber of commerce and other annual events that keep things hopping. Happy hour is set for 3-6 p.m. Monday-Friday, and T-shirts are available as evidence that you paid the place a visit.

WINONA

Here is a city with a lot going for it. It has its own 300-acre lake, created years ago when the Mississippi took a different channel. The lakeside is plotted in parkland that features a huge rose garden, athletic and recreational facilities, a band shell, fishing piers, and boat docks. Visible from the park is Sugar Loaf Mountain, some 585 feet above the valley floor. From nearby Garvin Heights, visitors can view the river for a distance of up to 30 miles.

The city has lots of picturesque downtown buildings, nice residential areas, a public and a private college, numerous golf courses, an aquatic center, ice rinks, snowmobile and cross-country ski trails, and venues for hikers and bicyclists. This town, with 26,355 citizens, produces everything from gummy bears to canoes in a part of the country that has yet to be overrun by developers.

For more information, contact the Winona Convention and Visitors Bureau by dialing (800) 657-4972, or (507) 452-2272. The WCVB Web site is www.visitwinona.com.

Bub's Brewing Company, Eatery and Saloon

65 East Fourth Street
Winona, MN 55987
Telephone: (507) 457-3121
Hours: 11:30 a.m.-1 a.m. (bar); 11:30 a.m.-10 p.m. (kitchen), closed major holidays.

Sure, Bub's is an attractive old building, one in which visitors can expect to kick back with a nice selection of beers. But it is also something more. Bub's (pronounced Boob's) was, from 1856 to 1969, a small local brewery. It no doubt arose with the coming of the railroad and the increased commerce on or near the Big River. Its demise was caused by the intense marketing practices of the big beer-makers.

Yet Bub's lives on, at least in name. If you enter this downtown Winona spot and ask, the help will show you a six-pack of Bub's in a display case. The proprietor bought the brewery's name for his tavern and restaurant as a nod of

Bub's Brewing Company, Eatery and Saloon, Winona.

respect to the longtime brewer. Ironically, there are several megabeers on tap, including Anheuser-Busch and Miller products.

Fortunately, there are many other tap beers from which to choose. They include a Bub's lager and a Bub's dark, made by Minnesota breweries exclusively for this place. And there are handles for several brands of Goose Island, Guinness, Leinenkugel, Schell, and Summit. Folks who hanker for wine or a mixed drink can have that, too. Happy hour occurs 4-7 p.m. Monday-Friday.

The food is pub food, but its quality and variety make it a pleasant surprise. "Anything I would remove from the menu would be noticed," says the owner. The big favorites are hamburgers and cheeseburgers, followed closely by chicken sandwiches and a variety of cold sandwiches. There also are soups and salads. Entertainment takes place only occasionally, there is no jukebox, and souvenirs come in the form of hats and T-shirts.

The mix of college students from Winona State University, folks involved in the city's retail businesses, tourists, local families, and just about everybody else form Bub's clientele. They come for the beer, food, pool, darts, computer golf, and foosball, but they also show up to participate in wide-ranging conversations over a cold brew.

"You don't have to be 21 to come in here, since it is also considered a restaurant," the owner points out. "I guess people like to come here just because it's very comfortable."

MINNEAPOLIS
and Vicinity

IMPOSSIBLY tall buildings, so high they dwarf the old, riverside grain elevators, are reflected in this "City of Lakes," with its skywalk-connected downtown and its 368,380 residents. A few years ago, Minneapolis was named the easiest place in which to grow, and that still may be true. Ideas for enterprise that are as fresh as a breeze off the prairie move around this sprawl of a town.

Other cities, such as Chicago and Milwaukee, were grain bins in the 19th century, but that was before wheat began to be planted in earnest from here west. Once railroads and river barges were in place, Minneapolis became, and remains today, North America's grain processing and transport center. Names like Cargill, General Mills, and Pillsbury have become synonymous with either milling or moving various kinds of wheat, corn, beans, sugar beets, and more. In the 20th century, high-tech firms, insurers, manufacturers, and marketers prevented the city from becoming a one-act town.

A pedestrian/transit corridor, Nicollet Mall, runs through the heart of downtown for a dozen blocks. Near all this shopping are Orchestra Hall, the Target Center, and the Warehouse District, the last thick with clubs, coffeehouses, restaurants, bars, and galleries. On the eastern edge of downtown is the Humphrey Metrodome, a big-league sports venue, and on the east side of the Mississippi River, but still in Minneapolis, is the main campus of the University of Minnesota.

Art galleries and museums abound here. The oft-whimsical Minnesota Sculpture Garden is a nice counterpoint to the American Swedish Institute, for example, where we learn of the determination of some European pioneers. The Minneapolis Institute of the Arts, on the city's south side, houses the state's largest collection of art of all kinds, from around the world. Another attraction is the array of lakes that dot all sorts of neighborhoods. These natural wonders contrast with the man-made Mall of America, just off Interstate 494 in suburban Bloomington.

Once virtually lily white, Minneapolis has taken on many hues and faiths with hardly a misstep. In addition to a growing Asian population, recent arrivals have included a number of Somalis. Obviously, the opportunities here far outweigh the adverse effects of the occasionally subzero weather. Culturally, Minneapolis is known as something of a pop music center, a place where a lot of publishing gets done, and the home of the renowned Guthrie Theater.

What do residents do in the winter? The number of cross-country skiing routes tells a traveler that this sport is an invigorating way to stay warm. Lots of guys have an old wood stove and a half-built hot rod in their garages, no matter what the age of the male or the age of his vehicle. Other male and female Minnesotans erect a shanty on a frozen lake and fish for walleye or panfish or whatever shows up. Still others content themselves with regular visits to the gym, trips to snowmobile country, or hikes in and around the south Minneapolis chain of lakes.

While there can be traffic tie-ups during rush hour, Minneapolis is an amazingly easy town in which to get into, out of, or around. East-west Interstate 94 and north-south Interstate 35 receive plenty of help from bypasses such as 35E, 35W, 494, and 694. Limited-access noninterstates whistle visitors through town on roads with numbers like 55, 77, and 100. Minneapolis–St. Paul International Airport, as an example, is literally a few minutes from downtown.

Frequently atop lists of livable metropolises, greater Minneapolis, with its vast range of suburbs, educated and enlightened workforce, numerous lakes, and mighty river, is a fitting metaphor for the entire state. For more information, call the Greater Minneapolis Convention and Visitors Association at (888) 676-MPLS or (612) 348-7000, or go to the Internet at www.minneapolis.org.

The Black Forest Inn

1 East 26th Street
Minneapolis, MN 55404
Telephone: (612) 872-0812
Hours: 11 a.m.-1 a.m. Monday-Saturday, noon-midnight
Sunday (bar); 11 a.m.-10 p.m. Monday-Thursday, 11 a.m.-
11 p.m. Friday-Saturday (kitchen). Closed major holidays.
Nearby attraction: Eat Street.

Are we in Uptown? Are we in Downtown? The Black Forest, the manager informs us, is in neither. If we must refer to an area location, tell prospective customers that this German tavern-restaurant is on Eat Street. Looking around, we see that the spot is at 26th Street and Nicollet Avenue. Which street is "Eat"? No matter where we look, there are diners, bistros, restaurants, and takeouts. What to do?

Here is one solution: Wherever in this neighborhood visitors choose to dine, they should drink their beer at the Black Forest. Not that there is anything wrong with the Black Forest's food. Those who enjoy Wiener schnitzel, sauerbraten, a Rueben sandwich, or homemade bratwurst should go nowhere

The Black Forest Inn, Minneapolis.

else. But if their hearts are set on Mexican or Vietnamese or what-have-you, this is the before or after destination for a brew.

The taps are many and varied: Bass Ale, Gosser, Grain Belt, Guinness Stout, Hacker-Pschorr light, dark, or weiss, James Page Amber Lager, Newcastle Ale, an oatmeal stout, Pilsner Urquell, Schell Light, Schell Dark, Spaten Lager, Summit, and several seasonal choices. From this long and varied list there has to be at least one beverage that hooks up nicely with any and all conceivable cuisines.

Another suggestion, at least in warm weather, is to enjoy the drafts in the adjacent outdoor garden. Though you and your friends are close enough to civilization that you can hear traffic, this spot may transport you to a vine-covered inn in rural Bavaria. Authentically dark inside, with a separate restaurant and bar, the Black Forest has a specific reputation, according to the manager. "Other restaurants are more oompapa. We concentrate on the food," she says.

Consequently, there is no jukebox and there are no entertainers to dilute the enjoyment of food and drink. Nor is there a happy hour, though visitors can reward themselves for having chosen this place by buying a souvenir T-shirt, a beer mug, a glass of wine, or a mixed drink.

The clientele when we stopped, between lunch and dinner, looked to be there on a beer break. There were a few tables of shoppers, a couple of professional and skilled fellows at the bar, and a regular who we hope lives within walking distance.

From downtown Minneapolis, the best non–rush hour route might be to head south on Interstate 35W, exiting west or right onto Lake Street. Drive west six blocks to Nicollet, then turn right or north and drive to 26th Street. The Black Forest is on the southeast corner, amid other restaurants with inferior beer menus.

The Borealis Restaurant

418 S. E. 13th Avenue
Minneapolis, MN 55414
Telephone: (612) 623-9541
Web site: www.borealiscafe.com
Hours: Always open (bar is open 8 a.m.-1 a.m.).
Nearby attraction: University of Minnesota's Weisman Art Museum, east bank of the Mississippi at Washington Avenue, telephone (612) 625-9494.

Had there been a spot like the Borealis (Subtitle: "Fine beer and wine bar") when we were in college, even fewer of us would have graduated. That is be-

The Borealis Restaurant, Minneapolis.

cause the modest, single-story site near the University of Minnesota offers more exotic brews per square foot than any undergraduate deserves or can handle.

Approximately half of the crowd at any given time is post or noncollegiate, says Dan, the general manager. Students and nonstudents alike are drawn to a dozen brands of draft beer, more than fifty exotic brews in bottles of varying sizes, an interesting and eclectic food menu, and nightly entertainment.

Pints of draft sell for $3.95-$6.95. There are levers for La Trappe (Belgium), Bass Ale (England), HB Weiss (Germany), Guinness (Ireland), and James Page (a few blocks from here). Domestic, out-of-state microbreweries get their due, with spigots for Sawtooth Ale (Colorado), Bell's Ale (Michigan), and Sprecher Black Bavarian (Wisconsin) also featured prominently.

Several of the liter-sized bottles, which are priced from $6.95 to $16.95, originate in Belgium. Belgians, by the way, consume more beer than anyone; tasting one or more of their products should tell a Borealis visitor why. Dan is especially proud of the fact that his emporium offers four different kinds of St. Sebastiaan's products: Bokrijks, Dark, Golden, and Porter. Some of the Belgian brews have been handmade by monks for centuries.

The smaller, individual bottles show equal variety, with prices of most premium beer from $3.95 to $7.95. Less expensive examples include Amstel Light, Bell's Pale Ale, Capital 1900, Harp, and four different James Page brews: Amber, Burley Brown, Klassic Ale, and Pale. The priciest single-serving bottle is English

Mead. At $16.95, a serving is for patrons of means. More common are Skull-splitter Scotch Ale at $5.95, Belzebuth at $6.95, and Delerium Tremens, $7.95. The last, by the way, is a Belgian beer with a heavy concentration of alcohol.

Speaking of which, moderate consumption is the key to success here, since the beverages are smooth and tasty but capable of delivering a wallop. After two servings, either dine or take a walk around the immediate, retail-intensive neighborhood, known as Dinkytown among University of Minnesota students. You will find kids occupying a few Borealis tables at all hours, though not all of them are swilling as they gossip or study.

Many are here for the kitchen, which is open constantly. There is a full breakfast menu, plus salads, soups, and sandwiches for lunch, and seven entrees for dinner. Omelets, hotcakes, Greek salad, Thai noodles, beans and rice, a Rueben sandwich, a turkey club, various burgers, pastas, chicken, and steak are among the offerings. Fare ranges from true vegetarian and vegan to the Borealis Feast, a 22-ounce, French-cut steak with potatoes and vegetable du jour. Thoughtfully, nonsmoking diners can call one section their own.

Because this rendezvous is perpetually open, there are two happy hours. All taps except Le Trappe are two-for-one from 8 to 10 a.m. and from 4 to 6 p.m. Entertainment is scheduled every day beginning as early as 4 p.m. and might be folk, jazz, rock, or classical music; there may or may not be a cover charge. The front door displays a tag of graffiti and a spot near the entrance shows a hole in the wall where an underage kid may have balked at being carded, but this is a safe, pleasant, and laid-back destination.

New in 2000, the bistro began life as a coffee-oriented café and evolved into a restaurant and bar (where coffee drinks remain available). Borealis is between Fourth and Fifth streets, four blocks southeast of Interstate Highway 35W, one and one-half blocks northeast of University Avenue, and about four blocks east of the Mississippi River.

Brit's Pub and Eating Establishment

1110 Nicollet Mall
Minneapolis, MN 55403
Telephone: (612) 332-3908
Hours: 11 a.m.-1 a.m. (bar); 11 a.m.-midnight (kitchen).
Closed Thanksgiving and Christmas.
Nearby attraction: Nicollet Mall, which but for Mall of America is Minnesota biggest shopping venue, runs for blocks, is reserved for pedestrians, and is right outside the door.

This place is a lot like our image of the average Brit: studiously disheveled yet sophisticated, quite likeable, with a lot of wit and appeal. Perhaps that is why the place is frequented by "comely up-and-comers," those svelte folks who have been out of college for a few years and find themselves paid well and respected for what they do in an office somewhere downtown.

They and the somewhat less fashionable, such as either of the authors of this book, gravitate to Brit's for 20 different brews. Obviously, Guinness is

Brit's Pub and Eating Establishment, Minneapolis.

highly popular here. But so is Bass Ale, Harp Lager, Newcastle Ale, and a great number of other beers and ales, most of which are brewed in the United Kingdom. On our visit, the temperature was not so cold that it destroyed the flavor of the beer, or so warm that it caused us to long for ice to plunk in our pint glass.

Virtually anything on tap goes well with fish and chips, which are ordered all day and into the night. This is a good example of the British standby; the chips are crisp, the fish is deep-fried but crisp and fresh. Other popular items from the far side of the pond include shepherd's pie and chicken potpie. The same menu is used all the time and for those who prefer, wine and liquor are available.

Something the more adventurous may want to try is Scotch eggs. These appetizer-size concoctions consist of a hard-boiled egg entombed in a ball of sausage. The sausage is dipped in breadcrumbs and cooked (we're not sure how) until the meat is done. Perhaps surprisingly, a Scotch egg goes well with a number of different kinds of pints. It is not, however, for those who obsess about their cholesterol count.

There are other British outposts in the Twin Cities, but Brit's offers one thing that no one else has—lawn bowling. Not *bocce*, the Italian bowling on the green, this is an old and authentic game played with a keen eye and a pint in hand. This particular patch (pitch?) of grass is on top of Brit's, where warm-weather diners and drinkers can sit and watch a vigorous game of bowls take place. One can bowl during the week by making a reservation; weekends feature open bowling. It's all quite fun—low key, nonmechanical, almost ecological in nature.

It should be mentioned that the taps here pump beers, ales, porters, and stouts with widely varying degrees of alcohol. For those who want to drink for hours and live to tell, Guinness is a wise choice. It is highly flavorful without being highly alcoholic. In contrast, English bitters, ales, and lagers may contain twice as much alcohol as any six-pack purchased for carryout. Being downtown obligates many of us to drive to our homes, so be careful. Perhaps a bit of bowling without grasping the pint will allow a patron to depart Brit's and arrive safely at his or her flat or cottage.

Bryant-Lake Bowl

810 W. Lake St.
Minneapolis, MN 55408
Telephone: (612) 825-3737
Hours: 8 a.m.-1 a.m. daily. Closed Thanksgiving and
Christmas Eve.
Web site: www.bryantlakebowl.com
Nearby attraction: Walker Art Center/Minneapolis
Sculpture Garden.

Bryant-Lake Bowl, Minneapolis.

This modest, venerable, bar-restaurant–bowling alley–theater is the top destination in the Twin Cities for celebrity spotting. We're not talking local celebs
here, but the kinds of people who star in first-run movies or whose names are
rattled off on "Entertainment Tonight." When they have a gig in town, this is
where they go afterward.

And why shouldn't they, since fame is not propelled by anorexia alone? At
Bryant-Lake Bowl they will find what has been termed the best beer list in Min-
neapolis. On tap are Grain Belt Premium, Newcastle Pale Ale, Foster's Lager,
Anchor Porter, James Page Amber Lager, Hop Ottin' India Pale Ale, Bass Ale,

Amstel Light, Summit Extra Pale Ale, Double Diamond, Pilsner Urquell133, Anchor Steam, Ace Pear Cider, Guinness Stout, Bell's Amber Ale, and Paulaner Hefe Weizen.

Drafts sell for $3.75 a pint or $2 per half-pint. There is an even longer list of bottled beers and ales, from Hopback Summer Lightning to Young's Old Nick. Many, many wines are available by the glass or by the bottle. Designated drivers can order anything from nonalcoholic beer to coffee-house coffees, tea, fruit juice, and unusual sodas.

This place also is popular with folks in the neighborhood. They grab breakfast here, gladly paying the extra buck for real maple syrup with their pancakes, French toast, or waffles. Or, they make this their luncheon destination to take advantage of sandwiches and burgers, vegetarian chili and other soups, nachos, or maybe a chipotle chicken plate. Evenings, look for entrees such as grilled flank steak and hash, pepper-crusted ahi (a fish), spinach, feta, and artichoke pasta, or noodly pad thai with a choice of tofu, chicken, or shrimp.

Between meals or after dinner there are some unusual offerings. How about warm fig salad, smoked trout salad, or cornmeal-crusted walleye strips? Choosing the best nibbles and the beer that goes with each could take a while. Some visitors actually bowl on one of eight vintage lanes in the back, while others attend the adjacent cabaret theater.

Not only can theatergoers avail themselves of some of the best new entertainment in town, the ones who show up 3-6 p.m. Monday through Friday can take advantage of the cabaret's happy hour! Drink and appetizer specials set the stage for comedians such as Ari Hoptman or singer-songwriters such as Leslie Ball. Upcoming acts when we visited included such interesting presentations as "Dial M (Minneapolis, presumably) for Comedy" and a tribute to those likable, talent-free punks, the Ramones. As Bertold Brecht is quoted, "A theater without beer is just a museum."

Back in the bar-restaurant, the patrons become more interesting as the night wears on. A fellow and gal who rolled up on a motorcycle may share a table with a swell and his date from the far, affluent side of Minnetonka. Beer fans come in with the reasonable expectation of finding their favorite brew, in bottle if not on draw. And with an ever-changing cast of characters in this area just east of Uptown, fresh faces mix easily with the entertainers on the prowl in the heartland.

Famous Dave's BBQ & Blues

3001 Hennepin Avenue South (Calhoun Square)
Minneapolis, MN 55408
Telephone: (612) 822-9900
Web site: www.famousdaves.com
Hours: 11 a.m.-midnight, Monday-Saturday, 10 a.m.-midnight
Sunday (kitchen); 11 a.m.-1 a.m. (bar). Closed major holidays.
Nearby attraction: The funky Uptown scene.

Not many franchises can be found in this book. Stated quite simply, we prefer the one-of-a-kind places. But when a franchise comes at us out of the blue, with a variety of beers, nightly entertainment, and decent food, it's tough to drive by.

The first Famous Dave's opened in June 1995 in Minneapolis, and restaurants can now be found in 15 states. Right now, there are 16 in Minnesota alone. Incorporating a standard menu and serving it with a roadhouse, northwoods lodge, or blues club theme, the rib joints have prospered to the point

Famous Dave's BBQ & Blues, Minneapolis.

111

that Dave finds his endeavors listed on NASDAQ. Musicians hold forth here, as well as at Dave's in Chicago and Memphis.

Unlike many of the franchises, this Famous Dave's has "a lot of levers" behind the bar to dispense tap beer. The big nationals are here in force, but so are Leinenkugel, Summit, Guinness, and more. A number of long-necked brews reside in the cooler, should you want a completely authentic drink with your ribs.

In fairness, food rather than beer is what put Famous Dave on the map. His specialty, natch, is hickory-smoked barbecue. A typical platter will include a diner's choice of barbecued meat plus a corn bread muffin, an ear of corn, and two sides. We especially liked the Wilbur beans, which were heavy with ham, and the whiskey-flavored drunken apples. Desserts, for those with large appetites, include bread pudding, Kahlua brownie, pecan pie, and ice cream sundae.

Sandwiches are stage-center at lunch. They include chopped pork, smoked ham, beef brisket, and pulled chicken with jack cheese. Soups such as wild rice and several side salads are available. Should diners have an ongoing hankering for Dave's barbecue, they may purchase sauce by the bottle here. His bottled sauces also are available in supermarkets. The restaurants are also good places to eat with the kids; "Lil' Wilbur" menus have half a dozen selections.

Virtually every evening from 9 p.m., decent blues music, offered by local, regional, or national fellows and gals, issues forth. Recently, players included Markiss and the Reggae-lators, Smokin' Joe Kubek, Lamont Cranston, Moses Oakland, the Superbenders, and the Willie Murphy Show. It isn't always blues—reggae, funk, Latin, Cajun, and more may be heard—but it is consistently worth a listen. Incredibly, there is never a cover charge.

Located on the first floor of the Calhoun Square complex, Famous Dave's is an Uptown fixture and a busy destination for beer drinkers who like a generous serving of the blues with their brews.

Gluek's Bar & Restaurant

16 N. Sixth St.
Minneapolis MN 55403
Telephone: (612) 338-6621
Web site: www.glueks.com
Hours: 10 a.m.-1 a.m. Monday-Saturday (bar);
11 a.m.-11 p.m. Monday-Saturday (kitchen).
Closed Sundays and major holidays.
Nearby attraction: Target Center, one-half block.

For four generations, Minneapolis residents and visitors have been heading to this handsome old spot for good food. Gluek's is among the chosen in this book because the menu complements beer better than anywhere else we could find in Minnesota. You like steamed mussels? Here they steam'em in Gluek beer. Looking for a beer-friendly sandwich? Order the Beer & Brat Special, wherein a bratwurst is steamed in Gluek beer and served with kraut on a sourdough roll—accompanied by a 16-oz. draft. In search of the ultimate beer-enhancing appetizer? Try the Essex, an array of domestic and imported artisan cheeses, sausage, and more.

Not only are the dishes here varied and flavorful, they are reasonably priced. The most expansive dinners are the dry-aged New York strip steak or the walleye pike, served fried in a Gluek beer batter or oven-broiled with a walnut-chive pesto; the tariff for either entree, with soup or salad, is $13.95. Every weekday, award winning

Gluek's Bar & Restaurant, Minneapolis.

Chef David Owen Jones, a frequent guest on local television cooking segments, brings forth a Blue Plate Special:

- Monday offers slow-cooked pot roast with mashed potatoes and vegetables.
- Tuesday brings country-style chicken-fried steak with sausage gravy and mashed potatoes.
- Wednesday presents an open-faced hot turkey sandwich with stuffing, mashed potatoes, and gravy.
- Thursday special is an open-faced hot roast beef sandwich with mashed potatoes and gravy.
- Friday offers an all-you-can-eat, New Orlean–style fish fry, with Cajun catfish, hush puppies, read beans and rice, and coleslaw.

There are at least three different Gluek Brewery products on tap at all times. Because the folks here know that customers cannot live by Gluek beer alone, they offer 16 other tap beers, mostly domestic microbrews. While liquor and wine are available, beer is the drink of choice among the vast majority. Staff members play their own compact discs; recently, before and after a Jimmy Buffett concert at the Target Center, the CD offerings were a wall of Buffett tunes. T-shirts, sweatshirts, and caps display the rampant red Gluek lion.

The menu befits a place with deep historical roots. Brewer Gottlieb Gluek arrived in Minneapolis in 1855 and set about making beer. Gluek products became so popular that the family built its own tavern, which marked its 100th year in 2002. The Bavarian beer hall look, complete with stained glass, vaulted ceiling, and exterior terra-cotta detailing, has been re-created.

The facility caters to a diverse clientele. Minneapolis residents in their early twenties like the place, and so do suits, who show up in appreciable numbers for happy hour, 4-6 p.m. Families who dine here may be from the city or just visiting, and events at the Target Center often have the place filled to overflowing. This may well be the most popular and well-known bar/restaurant in a part of the downtown long known as the Warehouse District.

Herkimer Pub and Brewery

2922 Lyndale Avenue South
Minneapolis, MN 55408
Telephone: (612) 821-0101
Web site: http://herkimerpub.citysearch.com
Hours: 11 a.m.-1 a.m. Monday-Friday, 10 a.m.-1 a.m.
Saturday-Sunday. Closed major holidays.
Nearby attraction: The allegedly hip Wedge-Uptown area.

Herkimer Pub and Brewery, Minneapolis.

In business only since late 1999, Herkimer is a brewpub where a visitor should look past growing pains and at the big picture. That picture is evident as one peers into the bar through the large front windows: Blake, the owner and brewmeister, is at work on lighter, longer aged, slightly more alcoholic German beers. The most flavorful are a delight, while the least flavorful seem flat and lifeless to fans of stronger brews.

The place exudes hygiene, from the tidy brick storefront beneath orange-and-green neon to the stainless steel tanks in back used for brewing. The bare brick walls are refreshingly free of bogus nostalgia. Even the restrooms are spotless, which always gains points in a beer drinker's book. The crowd is a collection of twenty- and thirty-something folks, arrayed at the bar, at tables, and in booths. The jukebox is better than average (Beatles, Beck, Jane's Addiction, Willy Nelson, etc.), and there is a long, wooden shuffleboard game against one wall.

While half a dozen beers are advertised, Herkimer usually has only two or three brews ready at the tap handles. We were there in the fall and put away an exemplary beer labeled Oktoberfest. Other brews were at best average. Blake has worked at breweries here and in Colorado. Beer drinkers are a patient bunch, so perhaps most of them will return when more taps are flowing. Those who run low on patience at the bar can take advantage of the fact that Herkimer also peddles wine and liquor. Happy hour runs 3-6 p.m. and involves two beers or two mixed drinks for the price of one.

The food is interesting and not all that pricey. Breakfast is available 10 a.m.- 2 p.m. weekends, lunch and dinner are served every day, and there is a special late-night, appetizer-oriented menu from 10 p.m. to closing that hits the spot with drinkers who need a little something rib-sticking. The best breakfast item may well be French toast with raspberry sauce. Lots of sides are available weekend mornings, including peanut butter!

Half a dozen varied items highlight lunch and dinner. They include a half or whole slab of ribs; chicken quesadilla; a Herkiburger (which is a hamburger beneath Swiss cheese, grilled onions, and a mushroom-sherry sauce); chop salad, with pulled chicken, shrimp, salami, lots of greens, and Italian dressing; a veggie sandwich with nicely grilled vegetables and two kinds of cheese; and desserts, from a banana split to a turtle ice cream pie.

Well after dark, appetizers may be warm, soft pretzels or other goodies that sit well with beer, such as fried zucchini, onion rings, sloppy joe or Cuban pork sandwiches, corn dogs, or nacho plates. This is a good place to hit after a concert or movie, as a number of nearby residents will attest.

James Page Brewing Company

1300 Quincy Street North East
Minneapolis, MN 55413
Telephone: (612) 378-0771
Web site: www.pagebrewing.com
Hours: Business hours. Tours at noon Saturdays
except holiday weekends.

For an operation with only seven or eight employees, the James Page Brewing Company is a most innovative place. Begun in 1986 by a fellow named James Page, the company was purchased by five old business-school friends in 1995. None of the five knew what they were getting into, but they were dazzled by the potential of a microbrewery.

That potential was a long time coming. First, the investors had to replace much of the brewing equipment. Second, the guys spent a lot of money on a new logo and on a billboard campaign while the beer was still not in many stores. Third, the master brewer fell ill and had to be replaced. And fourth, they learned that their packaging was so ugly that customers were avoiding the beer.

With changes in place, area residents actually began to enjoy the company's several brews. Between 1996 and 1998, for example, annual keg sales went from 2,700 to 6,300. The last four years have been marked by 50 percent growth each year, underwritten in part by the selling of shares to the public. In addition to employees, lots of local folks now own a stake in the company. Money raised has resulted in a spiffy new, in-house bottling line.

But it was a relationship with Minneapolis-based Northwest Airlines that has proven to be one of the nicest rewards so far. Page noted the airline's willingness to use local products on its flights and began to can two kinds of beer for in-flight refreshment. Sales of craft-brewed beer in cans—a real precedent—has resulted in more sales and greatly improved recognition.

Half a dozen products are created in a nondescript building northeast of the University of Minnesota campus. They include:

- **Boundary Waters Golden Lager**, made with wild rice, is a Pilsner-style beer sold only in bottles.

- **Burley Brown Ale** is an American brown ale available in bottles or on tap.

- **Finnegan's Irish Ale**, made with potatoes, is sold only on draft.

- **Iron Range Amber Lager**, a Vienna-style lager, it can be had in bottles, on tap, or in cans.

- **Klassic Alt Ale**, a golden, Cologne-style beverage, is exclusively a tap beer.

- **Voyageur Pale Ale**, copper colored and strongly flavored, also is available in bottles on draft or in cans.

Three of the beers, Burly Brown, Boundary Waters, and Iron Range, have won major awards at beer fests. The firm also has created a premium root beer, modeled after a brew made by a pioneering woman who lived boldly in the Boundary Waters area. A corporation with a conscience, James Page donates 2.5 percent of profits to local charitable needs. Is there a better reason to drink a beer?

Tours are given at noon every Saturday, providing the weekend does not coincide with a holiday. While there, check out the T-shirts, polo shirts, sweatshirts, jackets, denim shirts, caps, tap handles, glasses, and walking sticks(!). To find this place, head north from the university on University Avenue. Turn right or east on Broadway to Quincy.

Kieran's Irish Pub

330 Second Avenue South
Minneapolis, MN 55401
Telephone: (612) 339-4499
Web site: www.kierans.com
Hours: 11 a.m.-1 a.m. Closed major holidays.
Nearby attraction: The Hubert H. Humphrey Metrodome.

It is easy to read or sing or recite poetry and drink beer if someone else is doing the reading, singing, or recitation. That frequently is the situation at Kieran's, a downtown Minneapolis Irish tavern that modestly bills itself as "the home of Irish culture in the Twin Cities." It is that and more.

Past the handsome neon crest on the ground floor of the Towle Building, Kieran's is modern yet atmospheric, where almost every aspect of what an Irish pub should be exceeds expectations. There are eight variations of pints, from a Black and Tan (Guinness Stout and Bass Ale) to a Snakebite (Harp Lager and cider). The tap beer most prominently displayed is Finnegan's Irish Ale, made with potatoes by the local James Page Brewing Company.

Other tap brews include Bass Ale, Budweiser Light, Guinness Stout, Caffrey's, Harp Lager, Killian's Red, Leinenkugel's, James Page Ale, and Woodpecker Cider. Bottled beers include local stars such as Grain Belt and Summit, and overseas products including Grolsch from Holland and Foster's from Australia.

The long and respected list of other alcoholic beverages is worth reading, if for no other reason than that some care has been taken in selecting wines and liquors. At least a dozen wines are available by glass or bottle, including an underrated pinot grigio from Italy and a Riesling from Washington State. Several Irish whiskeys and a number of single-malt scotches are also available

The menu is encyclopedic. The Irish, bless'em, dine on stuff that goes well with a brisk drink. Examples range from appetizers such as salmon "roses" on fresh soda bread with lemon/dill cream, to potato-leek soup, to a roasted vegetable salad. Happy hour runs 4-7 p.m. weekdays. While the full dinner menu is available, savvy customers go for the appetizers, which include fish and chips, chips and salsa, onion wings, chicken wings, and Dublin chips with mayo and vinegar.

Specials are available Monday through Friday for lunch or dinner. Luncheon deals might be a bacon and lettuce-marinated tomato sandwich on sourdough, or a country ham sandwich on

This sign welcomes folks to Kieran's Irish Pub, Minneapolis.

wheat bread, topped with farmer cheese. In the evening, try bangers and mash with onion gravy or double trout filets, pan seared. There also are pub platters such as shepherd's pie and a trio of fish specials. Besides after-dinner drinks, look for double chocolate layer cake or turtle cheesecake for dessert.

Irish and English sports are fed live into bar TV sets. Most of the events are televised during the late morning, due to the change in time, and a small cover is charged. It is entirely possible to get away from the television, since there is a front bar and a lounge. Irish music, performed by the likes of Tommy Makem, the Sweet Colleens, or Four Shillings Short, can be heard live Thursday through Saturday in the front bar.

Happily, there are other events on Kieran's calendar (check the outstanding Web site for any day of the week). Poetry slams occur the second Tuesday evening of each month, and there are various readings and theatrical presentations on a regular basis. Travelers who harbor the urge to read or perform can do so during Open Mic nights, 8 p.m. Mondays, and dart throwers congregate at 7 p.m. every Tuesday.

By the way, there really is a guy named Kieran and a visitor can tell by his accent that he is the real thing. So, happily, is his pub.

Lee's Liquor Lounge

101 Glenwood Avenue North
Minneapolis, MN 55403
Telephone: (612) 338-9491
Web site: www.leesliquorlounge.com
Hours: 10 a.m.-1 a.m. Closed Thanksgiving and Christmas.
Nearby attraction: Target Center.

Lee's Liquor Lounge, Minneapolis.

Imagine this scenario, if you will: Two suburban couples roll into downtown Minneapolis with tickets to a professional event at the Target Center. It may be basketball or hockey or, for all we know, stadium motocross. They attend the big-time show, then take a chance on a squat, yellow-brick bar near where their car is parked. The bar visit, accompanied by great live music, is so rewarding that the four return the following weekend just to visit the tavern.

Lee's Liquor Lounge affects many people in that way. It is one of the very best live-music venues in the Twin Cities, a spot where the countless bands that come through from places like Austin, Texas, can expect a warm reception. Cover charges range from $4 to as much as $10, though $7 or $8 for a band with a growing national reputation is more the norm. Frequently there is no cover for local bands or a guest DJ.

ALL THE SUDS
that's fit to print

There are several ways to keep up on tavern news in Minnesota—besides occupying a barstool. First, all of the establishments in this book with Web sites are so noted. Second, new Web sites pop up all of the time; using the tavern's name, conduct an Internet search. Third, look for the following print media to supplement firsthand, at-the-bar knowledge:

• *Great Lakes Brewing News* is a tabloid published six times a year out of western New York State. As the name indicates, it covers brewers in states surrounding the Great Lakes. Minnesota has a page in each issue, where a knowledgeable fellow named James Lee Ellingson (e-mail Jim at james@brewingnews.com) provides late-breaking information. Copies are available free at brewpubs and breweries, or for $17 annually through the mail. For more information, contact *Brewing News*, 214 Muegel Rd., East Amherst, NY 14051.

• *Twin City Suds* also is a tabloid and it, too, is published six times a year. Put together in Milwaukee, where it is known as *Cream City Suds*, the publication carries more reviews and less breaking news than *Great Lakes*. The geographical area inside is slightly smaller, and includes what appears to be eastern Minnesota, all of Wisconsin, Chicagoland, plus stray reports from Iowa and Michigan. *Twin City Suds* is also a tavern or brewpub handout; a subscription is $24 annually. For more information, contact *Cream City Suds*, P. O. Box 1251, Milwaukee, WI 53201, or info@creamcitysuds.com.

• *City Pages* is the largest and most successful alternative weekly newspaper covering the Twin Cities metro area. Herein a tavern seeker can find ads and very brief reviews, particularly if the drinking venue in question offers either food or entertainment. Available at store entrances throughout Minneapolis or St. Paul, a subscription is $52 per year. This is the best single source for entertainment information for those who like music with their refreshment. For more information contact *City*

Pages at P. O. Box 59183, Minneapolis, MN 55459, or check the Web site at www.citypages.com.

• **Pulse of the Twin Cities** also is a weekly tab and a leaner competitor to *City Pages*. Billed as "your locally grown alternative newspaper" (*City Pages* is owned by *The Village Voice*), the edgier *Pulse* also is widely distributed every week. It contains a higher percentage of entertainment previews but only a smattering of food-drink info. Contact them at 3200 Chicago Avenue South, Minneapolis, MN 55407, or at www.pulsetc.com.

• **Mpls St Paul** is a monthly magazine that serves both cities. It indexes restaurants, a number of which are featured in this book. There are some reviews here, and a local chef delivers his opinions about what is good and bad in the regional dining scene. *Mpls St Paul* is available on newsstands for $3.50, or by subscribing at a cost of $19.95. For more information, write to *Mpls St Paul* at 220 South Sixth St., Suite 500, Minneapolis, MN 55402.

Contact Minnesota's Bookstore to see what is new in the way of reading material that may or may not mention new or existing taverns. The store is at 117 University Avenue, Room 110A, in St. Paul, or reach it by telephone at (800) 657-3757 or (651) 297-3000. Their Web site is www.minnesotabookstore.com. For vacation and tourism information about the entire state, including everything from the most remote fishing resorts to the rowdiest big-city nightlife, contact the state of Minnesota. They are at (800) 657-3700 or on the Internet at www.exploreminnesota.com.

But what music! If tunes are the best thing to accompany beer, these tunes will have visitors dancing, toe tapping, and upending 12-oz. bottles. There are no beers on tap here, but Lee's makes up for that omission by carrying a great many domestic beers, plus a few imported brews a music fan might like.

Lee's Liquor Lounge has not always been a musical destination. The present owner, Louie, was working full-time for the City of St. Paul Water Department when he learned that a bar in Minneapolis owned by the late Lee Tremer was for sale. Louie and his older brother bought the place and did away with the pool tables while improving the various lines of sight to the stage. Today, a seat at the bar affords a good view of the band.

First-time visitors should consult the Lee's Web site. There they will learn who is playing, what kind of music it might be (blues, oldies, rockabilly, swing, etc.), which band is opening for which other band, and how much it will cost. The music usually begins around 9 p.m. and, therefore, results in a couple of two-hour sets. The musicianship among these transient players is well worth the cover charge.

Recent talent booked at this spot on the west side of the downtown area includes Cosmic Slop, the Front Porch Swingin' Liquor Pigs, the Hillbilly Voodoo Dolls, the Vibro Champs, the Jaztronauts, Lazy Ike and the Daredevils, the Soul Tight Committee, Molly Maher and the Oakum Boys, the Mullet Club, Fair Weather Friend, Anahada Nada—we could go on. The crowd varies according to the type of music anticipated, but most folks seem to be between the ages of 25 and 40. There is a jukebox featuring many tunes by those who have appeared here in the past.

So forgive Louis for the dearth of draft and join him, the guys and girls on the bandstand, and the dancers on the checkered tile floor for a night of hot tunes and cool, if bottled, brews.

The Local

931 Nicollet Mall
Minneapolis, MN 55402
Telephone: (612) 904-1000
Web site: www.the-local.com
Hours: 11 a.m.-1 a.m. (bar); 11 a.m.-10 p.m.
Sunday-Wednesday, 11 a.m.-11 p.m. Thursday-Saturday.
Closed major holidays.
Nearby attraction: Shopping along Nicollet Mall.

The Local is the brainchild of Kieran, the same fellow whose name adorns another Irish pub a few blocks away. There are several differences between the two, all of them worth noting. The Local is larger, less event-oriented, more pretentious, but with equal emphasis on the quality of food and drink. Both appear quite successful, leading visitors to believe that Kieran, who was born in Ireland, is on to something.

In Ireland, "the local" in every town is the establishment with the best reputation for food, drink, and ambiance. The building in which the Local is housed was built in 1912. Its terra-cotta façade and high ceilings meet Kieran's standards for a "local" in downtown Minneapolis. The place gleams with terrazzo floors, crystal chandeliers, and ornate décor, and a whopping 80-foot-

The Local, Minneapolis.

long bar, divided into three areas. Parts of the informal pub were imported from Ireland.

Behind the bar you'll find 16 beers on tap. Guinness, as a drinker might suspect, is the big seller here, but trusted brews such as Bass Ale and Harp Lager receive frequent attention. Locally made Finnegan's Irish Ale, a potato product, also is on hand. One of the better deals is the vending of an Imperial pint (20 ounces) 11 a.m.-6 p.m. Monday-Friday for $3.50. Happy hour, 2-6 p.m. Monday-Friday, offers a reduction in the price of appetizers.

The atmosphere here is well above average. The back bar was designed specifically for this tavern and is a pleasing mix of handmade wood ornamentation and stained glass. Stained glass also separates the pub into two halves, with the bar on one side and antique tables and chairs on the other. Art ranges from a large mural depicting a café to Henri de Toulouse-Lautrec's paintings of the Moulin Rouge in 1890s Paris.

The menu is extensive. Appetizers that seem to go especially well with a beer or an ale include crispy calamari and mixed grill sausages with tomato chutney and cucumber salad. Speaking of salads, there are at least half a dozen. Perhaps the most intriguing is the farmers' salad, which contains grilled sausages, roasted mushrooms, greens, and sweet mustard dressing. Soups include potato-leek and chicken dumpling.

There are several ways to go in terms of a main course. Popular sandwiches may be pot roast on sourdough bread or the local burger with smoked bacon and Irish cheddar. Pub pies are available in roast pork and onion, curried lamb, and other configurations. Fish and chips, Irish lamb stew, steak, and salmon also are on the menu.

The bar in particular can be a very busy place. A number of folks who attend downtown events come here immediately afterward. Dartboards may be found on the mezzanine, and there are a couple of massive billiard tables for those who fancy the game. Gift certificates are available.

The Loring Bar and Café

1624 Harmon Place
Minneapolis, MN 55403
Telephone: (612) 486-5612
Web site: www.loringcafe.com
Hours: 4:30 p.m.-1 a.m. Monday-Thursday, 1 p.m.-1 a.m.
Friday, noon-1 a.m. Saturday-Sunday (bar); 5:30-9 p.m.
Tuesday-Thursday, 5:30-11 p.m. Friday-Saturday, 10 a.m.-
2:30 p.m. Sunday (kitchen). Closed major holidays.
Nearby attraction: The park and lagoon across the street.

Described as "tragically hip," on a postmodern block marred only by a Star-
buck's franchise at one end, the Loring Bar is most entertaining. The last time
we were there, a suitably spacey waitperson made change from a wad of cash
she kept in her cowboy hat.

The Loring Bar and Café, Minneapolis.

126

The bar shares the ground floor of a spacious old building with the Loring Café. Both are owned by a fellow named Jason, who says the bar has a European touch. The bar has a musty look and feel to it, what with sofas and occasional tables at occasional intervals. It is comfortable and—yes—hip without being pretentious. Jason says it is comfortable without having been consciously decorated, and he is right

There are eight beers on tap, all worth considering. Look for Summit Pale Ale, James Page Iron Range Amber Lager, Paulaner, Bass Ale, and Guinness Stout, plus three brands that change from time to time. Additional brews are available by the bottle, as are wines by the glass or bottle and mixed drinks.

The bar menu, which differs from that of the restaurant, is among the more unusual and rewarding a visitor will find. Appetizers that are especially beer-friendly include Edamame (salted soybeans with tamari dipping sauce) and golden chicken wings a la Atanalian. Featured items range from a Philly steak sandwich to a veggie burger, a New York strip steak, chicken, and ribs. Half a dozen pastas beckon, as do the pizzas, available with pepperoni, veggies, barbecue chicken, and ham and cheese

The dining room has fewer but more inventive entrees. They range from pork tenderloin to potato-encrusted halibut to sea scallops, Zather risotto, and beef tenderloin. Accompaniments might be a sweet corn emulsion, lime potato salad, jasmine rice custard, black pepper mascarpone, or carmelized Vidalia onion. The food here cries out for wine, but a committed beer drinker will throw caution to the winds and order his or her favorite malt beverage. A pungent and flavorful Summit Pale Ale, for example, probably goes down well with a number of dishes.

Who comes here? It's a cross section of in-town residents, suburbanites who feel daring, a few kids from the nearby art school, University of Minnesota students who want to amaze their visiting parents, and sundry others. Those others may include editorial staff members of a magazine called *Utne Reader*. The popular review of little-magazine articles is published in the same fascinating building that houses the Loring.

Stop the next ten people out the door and you will get ten different opinions on the Loring. Service tends to deteriorate in the café when it is busy, so perhaps the place to dine, as well as drink, is the bar.

Still want to have a drink here? Of course you do! The best way to arrive is to head north on Hennepin Avenue from Uptown. As Hennepin curves at about 17th Street, look for a right turn. That is Maple or 16th Street, and it curves around in front of the bar and café, which is on the right.

Lucia's Restaurant

1432 W. 31st St.
Minneapolis, MN 55408
Telephone: (612) 825-1572
Web site: www.lucias.com
Hours: 11:30 a.m.-2:30 p.m. Tuesday-Friday and 5:30-9:30
p.m. Tuesday-Thursday; 10 a.m.-2 p.m. and 5:30-10 p.m.
Saturday; 10 a.m.-2 p.m. and 5:30-9 p.m. Sunday (kitchen).
Wine bar serves food between lunch and dinner Tuesday-
Thursday and is open one hour after the dining room closes.
Closed major holidays and during the Uptown Art Fair.
Nearby attraction: Lake Calhoun, west on Lake Street.

Lucia's Restaurant, Minneapolis.

This is an American bistro, where the emphasis is on local, seasonal products and on wine. It is included here because very good beer is available and because other restaurants and taverns can learn something from the folks at Lucia's.

The smallish storefront in the heart of Uptown has been open for seven-teen years, but there is nothing stale or tired about the place. Customers enter

128

on the wine bar side of the building. Those with lunch or dinner reservations, which are advised, proceed to their tables. Drop-ins seat themselves in the wine bar area if they can find a vacant table. The dining room and the wine bar have separate menus.

But first to the beverage list. Beers on tap include Guinness, Hacker-Pschorr, and Three Floyds Alpha King. There are also bottled beers available. There are six red and five white wines offered by the glass, and more available by the bottle. Although most patrons order wine, beer is still popular and is served cold. Service is attentive without being intrusive.

In the dining room, regulars greet each other warmly. They are treated to a menu that changes weekly (and is posted on the Web site each Tuesday). Two recent entrees receiving rave reviews were pan-seared scallops in whiskey butter, and chicken breast with a Riesling wine–apple glaze, served with squash puree. Wine bar edibles include items such as foccacia and a thin-crust, spinach-topped pizza that works well with beer or wine. Lucia Watson, the owner, also is the chef.

Don't look for souvenirs, a jukebox, a Bob Dylan wannabe, or a sound system fuzzing the mind with Muzak. Besides food and drink, quiet conversation is the attraction. Live music is a classical guitar/cello duo and takes place only on New Year's Eve and on Feb. 14, which is both Valentine's Day and the restaurant's anniversary. The restaurant is smoke-free. Warm weather brings outside dining, and a valet parks cars in the evening in a lot immediately west of the building.

Nothing is inexpensive. Lucia charges fair prices for food, drink, and service that are well above average. It is a nice counterpoint to the racket of many other Uptown Minneapolis destinations.

MacKenzie's Scotch Pub

918 Hennepin Avenue
Minneapolis, MN 55403
Telephone: (612) 333-7268
Hours: 11 a.m.-1 a.m., open every day.
Nearby attraction: Downtown, since the tavern is about as downtown as a visitor can get.

MacKenzie's is a fraction of the size of the Rock Bottom Brewery across the street, and the parking lot next to this "American bar with a Scotch flavor" only looks as if it belongs to the bar. But those are the only things wrong with this downtown Minneapolis tavern that seems to do everything very well.

For starters, there are two dozen brews on tap. Most are ales of one sort or another. Though Guinness is the best seller, the folks at MacKenzie's introduce new, intriguing and/or seasonal beers on a regular basis. Look for seasonals such as Summit Oktoberfest, plus dazzling U.S. microbrews such as Bell's from Michigan and Anderson Valley from California. Manager George and owner Brian know and care about what they serve.

"There is nothing from Miller or Bud in the house," George reports.

Thought goes into the food, too. There is a lunch special every weekday that is a cut or two above the specials at many other places. Steak hot off the grill

MacKenzie's Scotch Pub, Minneapolis.

is just one example. Also popular are pizzas and build-your-own sandwiches, substantial to the point that they need no accompaniment (except beer). The pizzas are made here and then frozen; when needed, they are instantly defrosted and popped into the oven. Other foods include appetizers such as chicken strips.

The crowd here evolves as the day passes. Many office workers show up for lunch, to be replaced in the late afternoon with mostly fellows who either seem to be mid-level managers, or beer experts, or both. Patrons take on a slightly younger look after dark. MacKenzie's tailors its collection of compact discs to who is at the bar at the time, with soft rock in the afternoons and reggae or more hard-driving tunes at night. A number of urban tavern and restaurant workers rendezvous here after they get off work, proof that this is a swell place.

Brian and his father redid this 1850s building, which is attractive on the outside and atmospheric, with pretty stained glass, inside. There also are dartboards and a mild hubbub, but it is always possible to hear and be heard by companions. There is a full selection of liquor, which takes a back seat to the many draft beers and ales.

MacKenzie's is easy to spot—it is adjacent to the Orpheum Theater. The theater owns the parking lot previously mentioned, maintaining it for folks who want to stop and buy advance tickets. Should you park there at the wrong time, expect a towing bill of $100 and needless aggravation. Better to park a block or two away, if necessary, and walk to the tavern. MacKenzie's is worth the short hike.

Matt's Bar

3500 Cedar Avenue South
Minneapolis, MN 55407
Telephone: (612) 729-9936
Hours: 11 a.m.-midnight Sunday-Wednesday, 11 a.m.-1 a.m. Thursday-Saturday (bar); 11 a.m.-11 p.m. Sunday-Wednesday, 11 a.m.-midnight Thursday-Saturday, noon-11 p.m. Sunday (kitchen). Closed holidays.
Nearby attraction: Lake Hiawatha and Nokomis Park.

No human being can live on beer alone—or even on great cheeseburgers. Diners and drinkers witnessed a vivid example of this one night at Matt's, a corner bar in a blue-collar neighborhood a few blocks east of Interstate 35 West, south of downtown Minneapolis.

A delivery guy entered the tavern rather covertly, carrying large, insulated, keep-warm food bags. He and a bartender eagerly traded boxes of pizza for

Matt's Bar, Minneapolis.

boxes of burgers. That should tell visitors not only how good the cheeseburgers here are, but how easily they can become an item of commerce.

Before dissecting the Jucy Lucy, which has been called the Twin Cities' best burger, let's cruise the bar. Half a dozen beer taps point proudly toward the ceiling. They represent Grain Belt, Leinenkugel, Summit, Michelob Light, Michelob Dark, and Miller Lite. Scott, the owner and manager, says Grain Belt may be the best seller. He also notes that the spot has an unusually large number of domestic and imported bottled beers. Matt's opened its doors in 1954 and has always been primarily a restaurant visited by knowledgeable beer drinkers.

The Jucy Lucy, at $3.95 including tax, is a double cheeseburger. Don't be dismissive—travelers quickly learn that this is no franchise sandwich. In fact, it is the only burger that comes with a warning: The cheese has been sealed between the two patties of ground beef and, by the time it is cooked and delivered to bar or table, the inside is molten. Waitstaff or bartender will admonish customers to nibble around the perimeter for a while before taking the kind of chomp reserved for less volatile food. Keep a cold beer handy.

Served with a $1.50 portion of fries and a couple of $1.50, 8-ounce taps, the Jucy Lucy is an inspiring meal. There are, of course, other sandwiches at Matt's, but why not order the signature burger, especially during your initial visit? Speaking of visitors, the clientele is a mix of south Minneapolis residents and folks who grew up here and may have moved to an affluent suburb. Those Minnesotans can't find a competitive cheeseburger-beer combo just anywhere.

The jukebox has lots of capacity and is devoted to a wide range of music. Take the time to read the fine print and names of local bands from the recent past, such as the Jayhawks or Hüsker Dü, will pop out at you. So will nationally known rockers, blues musicians, and more. There are booths and tables, but residing at the bar means a traveler can see the busy grill guy at work. This is a popular spot for lunch and dinner, with at least as many fans as the Minnesota Twins.

Minneapolis Town Hall Brewery

1430 Washington Avenue South
Minneapolis, MN 55454
Telephone: (612) 339-8696
Web site: www.townhallbrewery.com
Hours: 11 a.m.-1 a.m.
Nearby attraction: St. Anthony Falls.

Located between St. Anthony Falls on the Mississippi River and the Humphrey Metrodome, the building that this popular brewpub occupies has been around since 1906. With its turn-of-the-last-century exterior, a mural on the side of the building, and 18-foot ceilings, the Town Hall is a pre- and post-game gathering place for folks with tickets to Metrodome events.

It is also a fine place to merely stop and sip. There are five brews no more than a tap pull away:
- **Masala Mama**, an India pale ale, is the hall's biggest seller. It possesses all of the strength and flavor one expects in an IPA, and it is crafted entirely with American hops.

- **Bright Spot Golden Ale** is a light ale, similar in intent to an American light beer—but without all of that low-calorie nonsense. The folks here call it their "introductory beer."

- **Black Water Oatmeal Stout** is as dark as an opposing team's collective heart. It is more alcoholic than, say, Guinness, and is made with domestic and imported malt. The concoction has copped awards and is a complex, rewarding drink.

- **West Bank Bitter** is named after the side of the river on which the Town Hall finds itself. This is a great intro to so-called English bitter beer, which

Minneapolis Town Hall Brewery.

is not particularly bitter. The English call the copper-colored brew "pale ale" when found in a bottle.

• **Hope and King Scotch Ale** is a deep amber and can be consumed with red meats and other highly flavored food without being overpowered. This version carries hints of chocolate, caramel, and raisin.

Making the scene on weekends means that a traveler can taste one or more cask ales, which are brews made here in small quantity that show their own flavor and character. There also are many single-malt scotches for sale, with Tuesdays set aside as Scotch and Cigar Night. Both the liquors and the stogies are sold at discount prices.

There is a separate dining room, where brews and any menu item can be ordered. We like the soy/ginger wings and chili cheese fries appetizers, the Greek and sesame chicken salads, and the chili, which is served beneath a generous dollop of sour cream and sprinklings of cheese and green onion unless you say otherwise.

On our visit, a customer nearby ordered a heart-stopping one-pound burger. Others content themselves with seven different, smaller burgers, and there are many other kinds of sandwiches, including meatloaf, pulled pork, and walleye. Pastas run the gamut, from unusual buffalo chicken penne to cheese tortellini. A couple of steaks are listed under the entrees, as are smoked pork chops and a fresh catch of the day.

There is a little something for everyone here, which may be why the clientele is a mix of downtown office guys and girls, students, sports addicts, visitors returning from St. Anthony Falls, etc. A fireplace, a sturdy pool table, several television sets tuned to sports, a brunch before each home Vikings game, and sidewalk dining in warm weather combine to provide this tavern with a high comfort level. To avoid crowds, it is wise to check on Metrodome doings before heading toward the Town Hall or other area bars.

Pracna on Main

117 Main Street Southeast
Minneapolis, MN 55414
Telephone: (612) 379-3200
Hours: 11:30 a.m.-1 a.m. (bar); 11:30 a.m.-midnight (kitchen).
Nearby attraction: St. Anthony Falls.

This oldest bar in Minneapolis is a classy place, from the setting to the building to the interior. The location provides visitors with a view of the Mississippi River and downtown, while the red brick structure dates from 1890. Small wonder that the clientele is a mix of the guilelessly well-heeled and the fairly well-traveled.

Step inside, past the 40-table outdoor dining area, and you will be greeted by a large number of beer taps, mounted midway down a sturdy and atmospheric wood bar. Local breweries are very well represented, with drafts from James Page, Summit, and Schell, varieties of which change with the seasons. In all there are 20 taps, so those who want an exotic, offshore brew will be fulfilled, too. In the cooler are ten bottle selections, including Corona, Heineken, and Rolling Rock.

Happy hour takes place 10 p.m.-1 a.m. nightly, with featured draft beers at $1.50 and discounts on all other drafts and on appetizers. Wine and liquor are always available. Quite a bit goes on outside, depending on the time of year. Fireworks displays on July 4 and New Year's Eve can be enjoyed from here, and the annual Stone Arch Festival takes place out front, with arts, crafts, and games. When we were last on Main Street, so were displays of exotic cars. The Minneapolis skyline makes for a dazzling backdrop.

Should food cross the traveler's mind, there is a complete menu. Sandwich specialties include the St. Anthony Falls Rueben and the 1890 (hot shaved

Pracna on Main, on the east bank of the Mississippi River, Minneapolis.

turkey with cranberry cream cheese and Swiss cheese on caraway rye bread). Appetizers, homemade soups, pastas, and entrees are available every day.

Customers come especially thick and fast from Friday afternoon through Sunday evening. We stopped shortly before 5 p.m. on a weekday and found a small but genial bunch at the bar, thoughtfully sipping quality brews. The variety is such that a visitor can drink his or her fill and never taste the same suds twice. Sounds like a plan.

As for drinking and dining outside, this may be the patio against which all of the other bars in the Twin Cities compete. The view, after all, is magnificent and the location, for many, is on the way home from work. From downtown, head northeast on Highway 65 (Central Avenue). Once across the Mississippi River, turn immediately to the right, onto Second Street North, and find a parking place. Pracna is one block back toward the river, adjacent to the St. Anthony Main complex.

Stub & Herb's Sports Bar

227 Oak Street South East
Minneapolis, MN 55414
Telephone: (612) 379-1880
Web site: www.stubandherbs.com
Hours: 11 a.m.-1 a.m.

Every college worth its sheepskins has one—a bar near the campus where generations of students have spent countless hours when they should have been in the library, the chapel, or the seminar. At the University of Minnesota, the heartbeat for Gopher fans is Stub & Herb's, billed as a sports bar but with even better credentials. It's such a quintessential college bar that travelers might feel nostalgic for the old alma mater, even if they dropped out of high school.

Two brothers, actually called Stub and Herb, opened the doors here in 1939. Since they drew their first beer, a lot has changed. For example, there are now 25 beers on tap and 55 beers in bottles. Tap choices include such local favorites as Grain Belt Premium and at least three different kinds of Summit, depending on the time of year. Though Hamm's is no longer brewed locally, the people who run this place somehow found it by the barrel and offer it to anyone with a little money.

Stub & Herb's Restaurant and Bar, Minneapolis.

Other tap goodies include three Leinenkugel variations; James Page Iron Range Amber, a microbrewed prize winner; Red Hook ESB; Sam Adams; Sierra Nevada; Caffery's Irish Ale; Heineken; Bass Ale; Labatt Blue; Newcastle Brown Ale; and more. Should none of these please a visitor, the bottle selection includes everything from Pilsener Urquel, made in Czechoslovaka, to Red Stripe, a Jamaican brew. Wine is available, and there is even a tap for margaritas!

Happy hour allows us to make the transition from drink to food. It is expansive, running 2:30-7 p.m. Monday-Friday and 2:30-5 p.m. on game days (football, basketball, and hockey). Besides drink discounts, there are food specials at the same times, involving such beer-friendly treats as french fries, waffle fries, buffalo wings, chips and salsa, peanuts, and pretzels.

The regular menu offers sandwiches and dishes named either in honor of the university's sports opponents, or after people with local ties. The Wisconsin Badger, as a visitor might suspect, is a mega-cheese sandwich, while the Jessie Ventura is a club sandwich, no doubt with extra ham. Clem Haskins, the former college coach who left Minneapolis under a cloud, has his name applied to grilled turkey, and Twin Cities native and ex-big leaguer Paul Molitor's monicker adorns the Rueben sandwich. Salads and soups look good, particularly robust bowls of beef stew and chili.

The décor needs no explanation to a University of Minnesota student or graduate. There are vintage megaphones, dangling pennants, photos of winning teams, and photos of individuals stars. Downstairs, pool tables are available, and they are surrounded by neon beer signs that all but overlap. The worst thing anybody has said about Stub & Herb's is that the building could use a little work. Considering the exuberance of collegiate fans, perhaps it's fortunate that the place still has two stories.

This destination is crowded to the point of insanity before, during, and after home games. It pays to check schedules before venturing into the immediate area, known as Stadium Village (though the old football stadium has been supplanted by the Metrodome). Should you show up anyway, the lack of parking will hint that, unless you have sports tickets in hand, you may want to raise a toast in a less crowded area.

WRIGHT'S TEN FAVORITE
Minnesota brews
(an admittedly subjective lineup)

1. Summit India Pale Ale. A must for those who are mortified by tasteless macro breweries. Tangy on tap, flawless in a bottle.

2. Bell's Pale Ale. Sorry, Minnesota, but as long as this Michigan beer is sold here, it will be near the top of the list. The bouquet alone should convince you.

3. Gluek Golden Pilsener. Gluek goes with food and food goes with Gluek. That is grounds for ordering another so as to complete a meal. Or just enjoy it by itself.

4. Grain Belt Premium. By the bottle or by the glass, this is a pleasant brew. And it is often a happy hour special.

5. Schell Bock. The New Ulm brewery should give lessons in how to make a bock. Theirs is yeasty and full-flavored, utterly unlike the sludge others pass off as bock.

6. James Page Voyageur Pale Ale. Another local beer that is hardy and full of flavor.

7. Mantorville Stage Coach Ale. Carefully made only on weekends by a couple of guys in a tiny town, this ale works by itself or with an array of food.

8. Pride of Pilsen. Available on tap only at Granite City in St. Cloud, this is a convincing Czech pilsener, brewed though it may have been by a canny Scot.

9. Sherlock's Home Bitter. An English brew served warmer than most beers, Sherlock's is authentic and has been praised by Brit beer fans here and abroad.

10. Lake Superior Pale Ale. This is an English-style ale as it is interpreted by a small and talented Duluth brewery. Most pleasing on tap.

William's Uptown Pub and Peanut Bar

2911 Hennepin Avenue
Minneapolis, MN 55408
Telephone: (612) 823-6271
Hours: 4 p.m.-1 a.m. Monday-Friday, noon-1 a.m. Saturday-Sunday (bar); 4 p.m. Monday-Friday, noon-midnight Saturday-Sunday (kitchen).
Nearby attraction: The Uptown scene.

A library branch stands across the street from William's. How many patrons, we wonder, have used the time before this pub's 4 p.m. opening to bone up on trivia there, only to lay away their fellow drinkers at William's with some arcane bit of knowledge? Here is our favorite factoid after having spent time at the bar: There are 70 different tap beers and more than 300 bottled beers from which to choose!

Imagine that. Customers can, if they choose, taste test, say, Bass Ale on tap versus Bass Ale in a bottle. Or they can sip a different beer every day for more than a year. The only problem with this embarrassment of riches is that people without a strong brand loyalty will find themselves to be terribly indecisive. But that's … okay.

Williams Uptown Pub and Peanut Bar, Minneapolis.

The crowd here ranges in age from just 21 to about 40. Offering peanuts with its brews, William's is a nice place to try beers you may never again run across. And the peanuts, if nibbled sparingly between beers, will keep the palate sharp for the next stout or ale or Pilsner. The most popular foods, which go well with any sort of malt beverage, include pitchers of spicy chicken wings, cheeseburger baskets, and spicy chicken sandwiches. Happy hour is 4-7 p.m. daily. Wine and liquor are stocked, but with 370 brands of beer, who needs them?

Mention should be made of the décor. This is a clean place, virtually devoid of rugs, cushy chairs and other items that might be repositories for dust or spilled beer. From the bright sign outside to the carefully maintained bar surface, it all strikes beer drinkers as a place that keeps its draft lines clean and its glassware shiny.

The building faces west, and it is brightly lit by the sun well past happy hour in the summer. Conversations are always audible since there is no music playing. Busiest time of the year? That might be in warm weather, when the Up town Art Fair closes off streets and attracts folks from all over. With William's standing guarantee of 70 tap beers and 300 bottled beers, consumers may not know art, but they most assuredly know what they like.

MINNETONKA

Minneapolis was founded hard by the Mississippi River for reasons of commerce. Had the reasons been recreational, there is no doubt that Lake Minnetonka would have won out. Huge and meandering, the lake today is the centerpiece for the city and several nice suburbs. Minnetonka, which means Big Water in Ojibwa, became a city in 1969. The present population is 51,301. For more information, contact the municipal government at (952) 939-8200, or go to the Web at www.eminnetonka.com.

Sherlock's Home

11000 Red Circle Drive
Minnetonka, MN 55343
Telephone: (952) 931-0203
Hours: 11 a.m.-1 a.m. Closed New Year's, Christmas.
Nearby attraction: Lake Minnetonka.

The Union Jack and the Stars and Stripes ripple proudly above this British brewpub, which, since its 1988 opening, has consistently rated among the best such spots anywhere west of the white cliffs of Dover. Michael Jackson (the beer expert, not the guy who sings and dances backwards) raves about the authenticity of Sherlock's Home products.

British beers and ales are crafted here, using all-British ingredients. The results are encouraging, as their seven drafts attest:

- **Bishop's Bitter** is light on the palate and has an amber hue and a bitter aftertaste. It has been called the best bitter in the United States.

- **Star of India** is, of course, India Pale Ale. It is bronze in color and has all the strength any regular IPA drinker could wish for.

- **Palace Porter** is thick and very dark, with an aroma of chocolate.

- **Piper's Pride Scottish Ale** is deep red, with a medium body and multiple complex flavors.

- **Staghead Stout** is almost as dark as porter and offers a coffeelike aroma and a bitter coffee finish.

- **Gold Crown Lager** is the most like American beer and the least like anything a drinker will find in an English pub. Nevertheless, it is a flavorful brew.

Sherlock's Home, Minnetonka.

- **Queen Anne Light** is a nod to local light-beer drinkers. It is named, with tongue firmly in cheek, since Queen Anne weighed some 14 stone (285 pounds!) at her death.

The brews are served at one of two temperatures. Stag's Head Stout, Bishop's Bitter, Piper's Pride, and Palace Porter are offered at 52 F degrees, while Star of India, Gold Crown Lager, and Queen Anne Light are served at 38 F degrees. The tavern notes that these are the respective temperatures of English and American cellars. All come in either the English pint (20-oz.) or half pint (10-oz.) glasses. If the seven standbys somehow fail to excite, it should be noted that Sherlock's also creates seasonal brews.

Some 75 items populate the separate lunch and dinner menus. The most in-demand meal is fish and chips, made with fish dipped in the restaurant's secret, ale-based batter. Other entrees include roast beef, shepherd's pie, and several curries. Purists can indulge in an incredible selection of single-malt scotch whiskies following a meal. It should also be noted that light food is available into the very late hours.

The décor here is a faithful reproduction of a Victorian public house and dining room. The massive bar and velvety dining chairs are designed to make a body feel comfortable in, say, a tweed jacket or an all-wool sweater. Owner Bill is British; his wife, manager Carol, is the daughter of a British couple who

143

migrated to the United States. Several staff members either are British or are capable of a convincing accent. The clientele is a mix of suburbanites, who may or may not be beer mavens.

Tours of the facilities are offered each Saturday at 2 p.m. It is best to call ahead and reserve a spot. English pint glasses in a set of four, with the Sherlock's Home logo thereon, are available as gifts or souvenirs.

Sherlock's Home is no snap to find. It is just off Shady Oak Road and just north of Highway 62 on the southeast side of Minnetonka. Red Circle Drive serves a number of retail establishments.

ST. LOUIS PARK

A western suburb close to Minneapolis, St. Louis Park is a mix of shopping, business, and residential areas, and is conveniently located near several golf courses. Interstate 394 defines most of its northern city limits, running east-west between downtown Minneapolis and I-494, which loops around the western side of the metro area. Highway 7, which stretches east-west through St. Louis Park near its southern edge, connects Minneapolis lakes Calhoun and Harriet to the suburbs that surround Lake Minnetonka.

Shelly's

6501 Wayzata Boulevard
St. Louis Park, MN 55426
Telephone: (763) 541-9900
Hours: 11 a.m.-10 p.m. Sunday-Thursday, 11 a.m.-midnight Friday-Saturday (kitchen closes at 11 p.m. Friday-Saturday). Closed Christmas.
Nearby attraction: Wirth Winter Recreation Area.

There is only one thing wrong with Shelly's, in St. Louis Park on the near-west side of the metro area: A less than observant traveler might mistake it for a franchise. Happily, once inside, there is no mistaking the food and drink that is offered. It is not cookie-cutter franchise fare.

We might not have come across Shelly's ourselves but for the recommendations of others. The up-north cabin facade, set near a chain restaurant, makes one think of multiple outlets. Pulling behind the place to park, the patio dining area is visible, as is the parking lot entrance. We stopped for lunch and found a steady stream of white-collar folks headed in.

Lunch, dinner, or before or after, patrons are greeted with a choice of 15 draft beers and a dozen bottled brands. The best seller on tap is Newcastle Ale, but it is closely followed by several Schell products, including the seasonally popular and tasty bock from the New Ulm brewer. Look, too, for names such as Bass, Guinness, Harp, and Red Hook on tap handles. Happy hour runs 3-7 p.m. Monday-Friday. Wine and liquor are also available

Truth be told, most people come here for the food. David Lue is the general manager and executive chef, and he has a growing reputation in this part of the country for straight-ahead, flavorful cooking. Diners around noon frequently ask for a walleye sandwich, a five-pepper beef brisket sandwich, or capellini, a vegetarian pasta dish. In the evening, signature meals center around the crispy half a duck, a walleye shore dinner, or a tenderloin filet.

The casual, northwoods lodge décor seems to complement the customers, who show up in anything from jeans to evening wear. A great time to discover Shelly's is after work on what is known as High Flying Friday. An expert shows up with lots of paraphernalia and puts on a fly-fishing lure-tying exhibition. The spacious restaurant includes a four-seasons porch for meetings and parties.

To arrive here from downtown Minneapolis, get on Interstate 394 headed west. Exit Louisiana Avenue, going left or south over the interstate highway. Take another left onto the frontage road, which is Wayzata Boulevard, and you're there. Sharp-eyed travelers will spot Shelly's on the south side of I-394 just before exiting onto Louisiana.

SAINT PAUL
and Vicinity

THOSE who do not know much about either place sometimes assume that St. Paul and Minneapolis compete with each other—and that St. Paul is the frequent loser. Such is not the case among the more knowledgeable, namely, the folks who make St. Paul home. Without thrusting out their collective chests, they are quietly pleased with their older city, which, after all, is the state capital and is seen to be less brassy than the larger, grain-based municipality to the west.

Now a city of 272,235, St. Paul began as a boat landing, presided over by a tough French fellow nicknamed Pig's Eye. He is said to have cast a disapproving glance at those who alighted and those who stayed aboard the boats plying the Mississippi. The name was changed from Pig's Eye to St. Paul in 1842 at the suggestion of a priest. With more miles of riverbank (29) than any other Mississippi River city, the town was bound to grow.

Being the state capital helped. So did being just down-river from a falls that prevented further river transport north or west. St. Paul was peopled by the Irish, whose labor brought rails to the city, and by Germans, Scandinavians, and a little bit of everything else. It is no accident today that the city is a major destination for recent immigrants such as the Hmong, who are from Laos.

A few years back, this was a place to lay low for everyone from bootlegging gangsters to an adulterous, middle-aged architect by the name of Frank Lloyd Wright. Evidently, the city had a reputation in the 20th century for being family oriented; the cops didn't look for crooks on the lam because there weren't many in St. Paul. Scott Fitzgerald, arguably St. Paul's most venerated resident, had to leave town to find the strata of high society that he depicted in his books.

A hard-working place, St. Paul also is the state's cultural capital. Theater and other arts are clustered around Rice Park, and the Minnesota Museum of American Art is nearby. The city supports a minor-league baseball team, a National Hockey League franchise, the Como Zoo, and several festivals, including the famed Winter Carnival. Shoppers love Summit and Grand avenues, and many pleasant, unassuming neighborhoods may be found merely by changing direction for a couple of blocks.

Numerous adjectives have been applied to St. Paul: clean, European, stable, progressive, cosmopolitan. It is all those and more.

Thinking about a visit? Contact the St. Paul Convention and Visitors Bureau at (800) 627-6101, or seek out Web site information at http://www.stpaulcvb.org.

Chang O'Hara's Bistro

498 Selby Avenue
St. Paul, MN 55102
Telephone: (651) 290-2338
Hours: 11:30 a.m.-1 a.m. (bar); 11 a.m.-11 p.m. Sunday-
Thursday, 11:30 a.m.-midnight Friday-Saturday (kitchen).
Nearby attraction: St. Paul Cathedral, a couple blocks
east of Selby.

By now you probably are aware that the east end of Selby is known as Cathedral Hill and is named for the magnificent nearby church belonging to the Roman Catholic diocese. You also may be aware that this once-proud neighborhood hit the skids after World War II and was retrieved from the wrecker's ball by people who like big cities and their neighborhoods.

Chang O'Hara's is on the south side of Selby, in a wonderful old brick building that once served as a fire station. Like other buildings hereabouts, it was redone, going through several alterations before opening as a drinking and dining establishment in 1993. Together with its spacious parking lot (a rare commodity these days), the venerable building is an ideal setting for a tavern.

Chang O'Hara's Bistro, St. Paul.

Eight different brews anchor the tap beer selection. Here a beer fan will find Bass Ale, Guinness Stout, Leinenkugel, Miller Lite, Newcastle Ale, Summit Grand, Summit Pale, and Summit Winter. Additional bottled beers are available, as well as wine and mixed drinks. Souvenir hunters can, for a price, walk out with a souvenir T-shirt or a sweatshirt.

An interesting time to show up at this tavern (Is it Irish? Is it Chinese? Is that a dragon on the sign?) is between 4 and 8 p.m. on Saturday evenings. A Dixieland band holds forth, providing the kinds of tunes that accompanied beer drinking on a regular basis perhaps a century ago. The crowd is slightly older than the daytime regulars, who run from their mid-20s on.

If food is a concern, the menu will reveal favorites such as pastas, burgers, hot and cold sandwiches, burritos, and appetizers. Thai chicken pasta is consumed in quantity, while the appetizer of choice, and one that should enhance most any brew is artichoke dip, served with crusty bread. Sarah, the manager, notes that diners can do their thing outside on the patio in warm weather.

She also assesses the crowd here as an interesting mix, especially during the day. It is an aggregate of neighborhood residents, state office workers, folks engaged in retail establishments in the vicinity, with an occasional visitor from out of town. Politicians, be they Democratic Farm Labor, Republican, or somewhere in between, have been known to stop here.

"This is a fun staff," Sarah says, adding that their good nature may be contagious.

Costello's on Selby

393 Selby Avenue
St. Paul, MN 55102
Telephone: (651) 291-1015
Hours: 11 a.m.-1 a.m. Monday-Saturday, 10 a.m.-1 a.m. Sunday (bar); 11 a.m.-9 p.m. Monday-Wednesday, 11 a.m.-10 p.m. Thursday-Saturday, 10 a.m.-5 p.m. Sunday (kitchen). Closed Easter, Memorial Day, Labor Day, Thanksgiving.
Nearby attraction: The State Capitol.

When Minnesota's controversial governor, Jessie Ventura, made an appearance on late-night network television as the guest of David Letterman, he was asked to explain the difference between Minneapolis and St. Paul. Jessie did not hesitate, saying that Minneapolis folks were apparently normal, whereas St. Paulites were Irish. "And you know about the Irish," Jessie said, making a guzzling motion with one hand.

Costello's Bar & Grill, St. Paul.

Evidently, the governor, whose office is just a few blocks from Costello's, saw something wrong in an occasional sip. The patrons here would disagree with their leader, since this is not only a place to drink, but a place to dine and to meet an incredible array of people.

"It's not unusual to see some of the state's top politicians at one end of the bar and St. Paul's most successful drug dealer at the other," a bartender confessed.

Perhaps that is a bit extreme. However, on one our recent visits, we shared bar space with a woman young enough to be our daughter on one side and a woman old enough to be our mother on the other. The former's friend was a woman who took obituaries eight hours daily at the *St. Paul Pioneer-Press*, while the older female was engaged in conversation with a middle-aged male, a professional musician. How's that for variety?

The employees here modestly describe Costello's as a "burger bar," because hamburgers and cheeseburgers, plus such good eats such as walleye appetizers, are consumed in quantity. The bar food is washed down with a wide selection of draft beers: Grain Belt Premium, Summit Pale Ale, a Summit seasonal, Bass Ale, Harp, Guinness, Newcastle Ale, Schmidt Golden Light, Miller Lite, and Budweiser. At least twice that many brands, some imported, are available by the bottle. There is a full supply of liquor, too.

This Irish tavern, which is really one big room, is in the Cathedral Hill Business District. In contrast to many boutiquey or otherwise pretentious places hereabouts, this is a down-to-earth destination. Slide into Costello's to learn about other lives and viewpoints. Is the truth a priority here? Does it really matter?

Don't look for a jukebox. Whoever is tending bar gets to pick the music, so his or her CDs are stacked into the player. The volume is audible but not intrusive, and the collective taste of the barkeeps is quite good. Costello's even has a small, adjacent parking lot, a nice extra on a subzero evening. The only thing that rankled us during an otherwise pleasant couple of hours was the thick cigarette smoke. Many would consider that a small price to pay for such a cosmopolitan joint.

The Dubliner Pub

2162 West University Avenue
St. Paul, MN 55114
Telephone: (651) 646-5551
Hours: 11 a.m.-1 a.m.
Nearby attraction: Endlessly fascinating University Avenue street life.

If you've had it with garish, ferny, or boutiquey places to drink, head west from downtown St. Paul or east from downtown Minneapolis to the Dubliner. Be sure to use University Avenue, which moves past the State Capitol and burgeoning Southeast Asian communities, eventually ending up in Minneapolis and Dinkytown, home of the University of Minnesota.

The Dubliner is on the southeast corner of University and Vandalia Street, just north of Interstate 94 in St. Paul. Turn south on Vandalia and look for a place to park. Inside this modest establishment is a simple, handsome, and tidy bar with a great many spigots. Before checking the beers and ales, be advised that patrons say the pints of Guinness here are the freshest and most expertly poured anywhere.

Not in the mood for a stout? Harp Lager and Bass Ale are equally available, as are several Summit beers and ales, Goose Island, and at least half a dozen others. The Dubliner sells spirits, but there is plenty of flavorful, much less alcoholic stuff from the taps. Pay for a pint and eavesdrop on a quiet conversation, then add your two cents worth. This is a great place to sit, sip, and chat about anything at all—by day, at any rate.

By night, the Dubliner is invaded by Irish or Celtic musicians. Tuneful, articulate, friendly, and quite talented, these folks either learned their trade in Ireland or they have spent years here practicing for this crowd, which is transformed into a noisy, mirthful bunch once the music begins. There is never a charge for the entertainment, which is scheduled as many as six nights a week. Take to the dance floor and learn a jig or a reel by giving either a try.

Neither food nor waitstaff gets in the way of a good time. Want a pint? Go to the bar and place your order. The service is friendly and quick, the beer is cold, and figuring out a tip is easy. (Remember, there is no cover charge. So when musicians are present, be generous.)

The crowd here, especially on Saturday nights, ranges from college kids to grandparents. Assuming the tunes are agreeable, much of the multitude will break out in guileless singalong from time to time. This place would appeal to your grown kids, your parents, your date, or your priest, in no particular order.

Instrumental work by some of the talent is nothing short of dazzling, as acoustic instruments pump out entirely adequate harmony, melody, and volume. Musicians are accessible during breaks; they are flattered if you ask about their style of music or their instruments. On Saturday in particular, many folks stay until closing. If they missed dinner, the free popcorn absorbs enough liquid to see them safely home.

Great Waters Brewing Company

426 St. Peter Street
St. Paul, MN 55102
Telephone: (651) 224-2739
Hours: 11 a.m.-1 a.m. Monday-Saturday, noon-1 a.m. Sunday (bar); 11 a.m.-11 p.m. (kitchen). Closed Thanksgiving and Christmas.
Nearby attraction: Several theaters, including the Fitzgerald, within walking distance.

A casual observer might think the best reason to meet at Great Waters is that it is only a short hike from the Fitzgerald Theater, where the inimitable Garrison Keillor frequently spends Saturday evenings presenting the public radio show, "A Prairie Home Companion." While that is a great excuse, there are a couple of additional reasons to meet here in downtown St. Paul.

First, this unassuming building has a bit of history to it. It is known as the Hamm building, because it was owned by the same family that brewed the once-mighty beer that featured a dancing bear and a "from the land of sky-blue waters" theme. Second, speaking of water, there is a 1,500-ft. deep well inside Great Waters. As you may have guessed, the folks here use it to make beer.

Great Waters Brewing Company, St. Paul.

There are eight different beers here, or two kinds of four, explains owner Sean O'Byrne.

"We have four colder beers on tap and four cask-conditioned ales, which are kept and drunk at a warmer temperature." One result of this dichotomy has been awards. The Real Ale Fest in Chicago recently bestowed a medal on Great Waters, indicating that these people know and care about what they are making here. Yes, you can order wine or a mixed drink if, for some strange reason, you fear beer.

The menu here looks quite complete, with items such as a Rueben sandwich and a Cajun burger for lunch, or a filet mignon for dinner. The soups, the salad dressings, and the desserts are made from scratch. For those who don't want beer for dessert, Sean endorses the coconut chocolate chip bread pudding.

Several other things are worth mentioning. Designated drivers can toast their passengers with homemade root beer. There are two happy hours, 3:30-6:30 p.m. Monday-Friday and 10:30 p.m. to closing every night but Saturday. The patio seats 50 in warm weather, and both the bar and the dining area are comfortable while still looking stylish.

156

In business since 1997, Great Waters is just south of Seventh Street (Highway 5). St. Peter is a one-way street, heading south toward a bend in the Mississippi, some two blocks away. If you reach Kellogg Boulevard on St. Peter, you have gone too far south. Turn left twice and you are headed back north on Wabasha Avenue. A left at Sixth Street (Fifth Street is one way the wrong way) and a left again at St. Peter will put you very near Great Waters—and the products that come from that 1,500-foot-deep well.

Green Mill Brewing Company

57 South Hamline Avenue
St. Paul, MN 55105
Telephone: (651) 698-0353
Hours: 11 a.m.-1 a.m. Monday-Saturday, 11 a.m.-midnight Sunday (bar); 11 a.m.-midnight Monday-Saturday, 11 a.m.-11 p.m. Sunday (kitchen).
Web site: www.greenmill.com
Nearby attraction: The parklike banks of the Mississippi River.

You may recall the first time you tasted pizza. As a 12-year-old Hoosier, the elder author of this book found himself in Pittsburgh with a lush, gloppy, spicy slice. It was "foreign, exotic" food, almost too good. Pizza began to show up in earnest in the Midwest in the late 1950s. We assumed it was something GI's had tasted during the occupation of Italy in World War II and brought back with them.

We were, of course, dead wrong, and the Green Mill's history proves it. The Mill was a soda shop in the 1930s that served pizza and other homemade delights. After a change in ownership, deep-dish, Chicago-style pizza was introduced in 1976. The recipe came from the family of one of the owners. These Italian-Americans had been enjoying homemade pies for decades. Pizzas that could compete with anything in Sicily or beyond were introduced to non-Italians in places like this. This Green Mill restaurant is the original, just off Grand Avenue. It is also unlike any of the other Green Mills in Minnesota and elsewhere, since this one brews its own beer.

Green Mill Pale Ale is the most popular of half a dozen different brews available. Five flavors stay the same and one is seasonal. It is a mark of confidence in their brews that this brewpub-restaurant offers only one bottled beer, Bud Light. There is a full bar (wine goes well with pizza, of course), music choices are courtesy of satellite, and customers may purchase T-shirts or sweatshirts.

Green Mill Brewing Company, St. Paul.

This Green Mill offers three kinds of pizza plus some specialty 'zas, which accounts for the fact that the carryout business here is brisk. The thin-crust pizza goes especially well with the heartiest ales; the hand-tossed accommodates a range of beers; and the rich, deep-dish pizza is a valid excuse to go for a bottled light beer if you must. All pizzas are made from scratch, and the menu admonishes that the pies take 20-40 minutes to make and bake. What better excuse for another round?

Toppings include all a visitor might expect, plus a choice of three kinds of tomatoes, spicy chicken, goat cheese, prosciutto, and fresh spinach. Specialty pizzas run the gamut, from a garlic-roasted potato pizza to a pizza created with four different cheeses. Luncheon specials include lasagna, tortellini, fettucine, spaghetti, penne pasta with wild mushrooms, and pizza by the slice. The menu also offers everything from appetizers to sandwiches to soups, salads, and desserts.

Minnesota Brewing Company

882 West Seventh Street
St. Paul, MN 55102
Telephone: (651) 290-8209
Web site: www.grainbelt.com
Hours: 1 p.m. Tuesday-Friday (tours).
Nearby attraction: The old neighborhood.

Now this is a brewery! If all you younger beer drinkers have seen is either a modern brewpub or a modern microbrewery, come on down. The Minnesota Brewing Company has castlelike ramparts, craggy old brick buildings, a spring that brings up water from deep within the earth, and a series of brands well worth tasting.

But first a bit of history. This was originally the Cave Brewery, founded in 1855 and so named because cool underground caves were used to lager or age the beer. The brewery was sold in 1900 and became the Jacob Schmidt Brewing Company, brewers of Schmidt Beer. The place changed hands several times beginning in 1955, ending up the property of the G. Heileman Brewing Company of LaCrosse, Wisconsin. The St. Paul site was closed in 1990 and demolition was scheduled for the following year.

But then, a group of investors reopened and renamed the brewery in 1991. They acquired the Grain Belt brand in 1994 and have experienced marked success ever since. Now the 12th largest U.S. brewery, Minnesota Brewing Company produces more than a dozen interesting brews. They include:

- **Grain Belt Premium.** The flagship beer has experienced greatly increased sales since winning a gold medal among lagers at the Great American Beer Festival a few years back. It is the only product offered in a clear, long-neck bottle.

- **Golden Grain Belt.** The company's brewers have attempted to recapture the taste of the first post-Prohibition brew. Taste and guess if they succeeded.

- **Golden Grain Belt Light.** The light version of the brand.

- **Pig's Eye Pilsner.** First made in 1992, this medium-bodied Pilsner beer is named after Pig's Eye Parrant, said to be the somewhat nefarious founder of St. Paul.

- **Pig's Eye Lean.** Pale gold, highly carbonated, and containing only 112 calories, this is for beer drinkers watching their weight.

- **Pig's Eye Ice.** Slightly more alcoholic than its peers, this beer is made with a process that freezes the water at a precise moment.

- **Pig's Eye Red Amber.** A medal winner, this brew is made from special malts and caramel hops.

159

- **Pig's Eye N.A..** Another medal winner, N.A. is virtually (approximately 99.5 percent) free of alcohol.

- **Brewer's Cave Black Barley.** Handcrafted mixing of barley wheat and Vienna malt give this beer its distinct flavor.

- **Brewer's Cave Golden Caramel.** A lager, Golden Caramel is created by joining barley and caramel malts.

- **Brewer's Cave Amber Wheat.** This is a black barley ale that ends up with a rich, chestnut-roasted hue and a nutty flavor.

The brewers use water from what is said to be the deepest aquifer in North America. Some 1,100 feet down and 37,000 years old, this reservoir has been tapped by the brewery since the 19th century. By the way, purchasing a container of this water at the entrance to the plant will add to a fund that aids needy residents of West Seventh Street, the city's so-called West End.

Minnesota Brewing Company, St. Paul.

Anyone who can't find a beer he or she likes from Minnesota Brewing's menu simply is not a beer drinker. Grain Belt Premium, for example, has shouldered its way into a great many Minnesota bars, simply because it tastes great and has a long-familiar name. The company also brews three different lemon-flavored alcoholic beverages, and it stands ready to contract brew for anyone with a good formula and good credit. With a nod to objectivity, it should also be noted that ethanol is made here and that the odor from its episodic production has incensed neighbors and city officials.

Tours take place at 1 p.m, Tuesday through Saturday. Call (651) 290-8209 to reserve your place. The tour ends in a large rathskeller, where samples are provided. The rathskeller is outfitted with seating for 80 and features contemporary electronics. Hold a family reunion here, with Grain Belt and other refreshments, and your family will thank you for generations to come.

Summit Brewing Company

910 Montreal Circle
St. Paul, MN 55102
Telephone: (651) 265-7800
Web site: www.summitbrewing.com
Hours: Tours are 1 p.m. Tuesday, Thursday, and Saturday (no tours holiday weekends).
Nearby attraction: Downtown St. Paul.

Summit Brewing Company, St. Paul.

A bartender of our acquaintance, given neither to hollow praise nor exaggeration, grants the Summit Brewing Company high marks. "Those guys are good," she says as she pulls on a Summit handle, one of eight taps in her Madison, Wisconsin, tavern. "Everything they make is worth trying."

YESTERDAY'S BREWERY
is tomorrow's . . . ?

Visitors to St. Paul who wander around the northeast side may drive beneath an arch on Payne Avenue that piques their interest. The walkway connects two venerable buildings and displays a one-word sign: Stroh's. Thereby hangs a bittersweet, beer-oriented tale ...

The Hamm family began in the 19th century to make beer in St. Paul near the railroad corridor that ran northeast along Phalen Creek from downtown. For years and years, Hamm's was consumed and enjoyed in the upper Midwest, from Chicago well into the Dakotas. But hard times eventually befell the brand and the brewery was sold to the equally respected Stroh Brewing Company of Detroit in the 1980s.

Stroh, at the time, was the nation's third largest maker of beer. Stroh's was, for example, the best-selling brand in Michigan and Ohio, two states with large populations. By buying the Hamm plant, Stroh hoped to increase capacity. Like many other beers, however, Stroh and its several brands eventually were outsold by the megamarketers, Anheuser-Busch, Coors, and Miller. With excess capacity in an aging facility, Stroh closed the Hamm brewery in September 1997. In May 1999, Stroh ceased making beer, selling its brand names to Pabst.

According to St. Paul city planners and developers, some of the buildings in the brewery complex will be saved if they are of historical or architectural interest. Other structures, such as the grain elevators, have already been razed. "We redeveloped both ends of the corridor. Now we need to develop the area in between," a spokesperson noted.

Boy, have they. The brewery is occupied at the moment with active (small offices) and passive (storage) activities. In the same area, a vast site that once was the spot where Whirlpool refrigerators were made is now a slag heap where asphalt is recycled. The remaining brewery buildings have magnificent views of downtown St. Paul and the Mississippi River gorge. The ultimate use of this area, which will be called Phalen Boulevard, is yet to be decided.

The odds of another brewery are slim indeed. So when visitors pass beneath the arch, they should shed a tear for two widely respected but nonexisting beers. Though the names can still be found on bottles and cans, neither original Stroh's, which was "fire brewed," nor original Hamm's, "from the land of sky-blue waters," will ever quench another thirst.

Seven different English or German-style brews with regional respect are produced by the modern little brewery just off West Seventh Avenue (State Route 5) in St. Paul. They include:

- **Summit Extra Pale Ale.** This is the company's flagship product, light bronze in color, with a pronounced hoppy flavor. A British-style ale, it is 5.4 percent alcohol by volume.

- **Summit Great Northern Porter.** Dark in color but lighter-bodied than many drinkers expect, Summit's answer to Guinness is a malty concoction. Alcohol content is 4.9 percent.

- **Summit India Pale Ale.** First brewed in 18th-century England and designed to survive long voyages to India, this version is 6.3 percent alcohol. While taking the tour, ask why this is a "dry hopped" ale.

- **Summit Hefe Weizen.** A unique flavor and a cloudy appearance are the result of using authentic German weizen yeast. Also contributing to the taste and aroma is a large helping of malted wheat. Suggested to be served with a slice of lemon, Hefe Weizen contains 4.7 percent alcohol.

- **Summit Heimertingen Maibock.** Available only in April and May, Maibock or May Beer is a malty, pale bock brewed with German lager yeast. Heimertingen has an alcohol content of 7 percent, and proves that not all bock beer is dark.

- **Summit Dusseldorf Style Alt Bier.** Sold in the fall, this rich, malted beer employs the same kind of top fermentation advocated by brewers in the Dusseldorf region of Germany. Alcohol content is 5.2 percent.

- **Summit Winter Ale.** Brewed and sold during cold weather, this burgundy-colored, slightly spicy winter warmer is the kind of hardy drink that is at home around a fireplace. Alcohol content is 5.5 percent.

The brewery began life in 1986 on University Avenue in St. Paul. In 1998, after slow but steady growth, brewers moved into their new digs virtually within sight of the Mississippi River. Unlike the big guys, Summit uses only four ingredients in its beers: filtered water, malt, hops, and yeast. No barley, no corn, no rice, no kidding. It's the way these ingredients go together, the beer-making recipe, that results in seven distinct brews.

Reservations are requested for a tour. Once inside the brewery, visitors will see big copper kettles, a tasting room, a place to purchase souvenirs, and quantities of freshly brewed Summit being put into kegs or bottles for delivery. As far away as the parking lot, folks will detect the distinct, grainy aromas that tell them this is a seductive way to use the hop harvest.

The brewery is two blocks south of West Seventh Street and about a block east of I-35E. Drivers heading north on the interstate highway and exiting east onto West Seventh Street can take the first right, which is Montreal Way. The street leads through a small business park to Montreal Circle and the parking lot on the west side of Summit's green-roofed building.

Sweeney's Saloon & Café

96 North Dale Street
St. Paul, MN 55102
Telephone: (651) 221-9157
Hours: 11 a.m.-1 a.m. (bar); 11 a.m.-11 p.m. Monday-Thursday, 11 a.m.-midnight Friday-Saturday (kitchen).
Nearby attraction: The State Capitol.

Conviviality makes Sweeney's easy to misread. Because the crowd here is friendly, willing to talk to both friends and strangers, attentive to which sport may be on TV, and interested in drinking good beer, the folks may be mistaken for a homogeneous bunch. Such is not the case, as a bartender recently pointed out.

"It's funny," he said. "Some evenings it will be all thirty-somethings, on other evenings it will be all ages. And there are nights when several college kids come here." (Besides the University of Minnesota, with campuses in both cities, St. Paul is the site of a good number of private colleges.)

Regardless, the patrons appreciate one of the nicest selections of tap beers anywhere. Loyalty must play a part, because St. Paul's respected Summit Brewing Company has every one of its tap beers represented. Those who are looking for other brews can choose from Leinenkugel, Leinenkugel Honey Weiss, Bass Ale, Harp, Guinness, Newcastle Ale, Sam Adams, Hard Core Cider, Bud

Sweeney's Saloon & Café, St. Paul.

Light, and Miller Lite. Summit's several stalks seem to get a lot of play here. Wine and mixed drinks also sell briskly.

Sweeney's, in an old brick storefront building just north of St. Paul's fashionable Grand and Summit avenues, has a large lunch-and-later crowd. The most popular luncheon special may be the Buckburger, which has been on the menu for a long time and sells for $2—a real bargain for a made-to-order sandwich. Other popular treats include the pastrami–and–jack cheese stacker, chili, and flamingo wings. Food is served at both bar and table.

Earlier we mentioned conversation, something that continues nonstop here. Televised sports are turned down, and the CD collection plays at an audible but not overpowering volume. Speaking of which, customers are encouraged to bring in a favored compact disc. It will be shared with the house, and played along with the CDs belonging to the bar.

Behind the old structure is a parking lot. There is room outside for patio dining in warm weather.

The downside of Sweeney's is that, on weekend evenings, the place is packed. The upside is that those in the throng tend to be friendly, willing to talk and listen about any subject anybody cares to bring up.

Tavern on Grand

656 Grand Avenue
St. Paul, MN 55105
Telephone: (651) 228-9030
Hours: 11 a.m.-11 p.m. (kitchen); 11 a.m.-1 a.m. (bar). Closed
Thanksgiving, Christmas.
Nearby attraction: James J. Hill House.

Why are so many fish dinners complemented with beer? Is it because of the
number of fishermen and women who are beer drinkers? Is it because someone once spilled a beer in deep-fried fish batter and liked the taste? Or is it because fish is a light entrée, leaving room for a fair amount of suds? Not only
do we not know the answer, we don't even know which freshwater fish is the
most flavorful.

Three of North America's tastiest freshwater varieties are well represented in
Minnesota. Downriver from the Twin Cities, folks swear by catfish, which seem
to increase in size as the river grows wider. Gopher State residents who regularly fish the many small lakes are loyal to perch, not minding that it may take

Tavern on Grand, St. Paul.

a couple dozen specimens to feed four people. Still others prefer to dine on the walleye pike, a fighting game fish that, in fact, is part of the perch family.

The folks at Tavern on Grand side with walleye fishers. The restaurateurs have been preparing fried and broiled walleye for lunch and dinner as long as most shoppers on this, St. Paul's hippest street, can recall. Lest you doubt their intent, check out that fishy profile above the front door. And above the fish, emblazoned in neon, are these words: "Famous for Walleye."

Offering either a bar or a dining area, the Tavern on Grand provides fish eaters with these tap-beer choices: Budweiser, Guinness, Leinenkugel, Michelob Golden Light, Miller Lite, Paulaner, Red Hook, and three varieties of Summit. There also are a decent number of bottled brands available, as well as a selection of wine and liquor.

For those who like their brews with something more substantial than fish, this tavern also offers items such as steaks and ribs. There is no jukebox or piped-in music to intrude on the dining experience, which is enjoyed at least as much by families as by anyone else. Those who want to advertise that they have dined here can score a T-shirt, but the Tavern doesn't push such memorabilia.

Nor do they get their fresh walleye with a hook, line, and sinker. Walleye, now in demand in such exotic locales as Illinois and Indiana, are raised on fish farms. Happily, fish farming can satisfy the craving. Anyway, selling game fish is illegal.

Securing a walleye outside a restaurant or a grocery store is left to the committed angler. Minnesota's north-central lakes—Lake of the Woods, Leech, Mille Lacs, Winnibigoshish, etc.—are termed "walleye factories" by the state. But besides a $17 license and a long drive, the walleye seeker has to be in the right place, with the right bait, at the right time (often before sunrise). It is way easier to slide into the Tavern on Grand and hook your catch with a cold draft on the side.

Vine Park Brewing Company

242 West Seventh Street
St. Paul, MN 55102
Telephone: (651) 228-1355 (brewery);
228-1358 (pub and beer garden)
Web site: www.vinepark.com
Hours: noon-8:30 p.m. Tuesday-Friday, 9 a.m.-6 p.m.
Saturday, closed Sunday-Monday (brewery); 11 a.m.-1 a.m.
Tuesday-Saturday, 10 a.m.-10 p.m. Sunday, closed Monday
(pub and beer garden).
Nearby attraction: Downtown St. Paul.

This place has a couple of surprises, all of them pleasant. On entering, visitors learn that they can brew their own beer, complete with labeled bottles that prove they did it, on the premises. Or, they can patronize the pub and beer garden for beer brewed by the people who do it here for a living. Should they order food, they may understand why *Mpls St. Paul* magazine recently proclaimed this "the best brewpub fare in town."

The idea for opening a brew-on-premises (BOP) establishment came to David and Allyson in 1995, after they had visited successful operations on the

Vine Park Brewing Company, St. Paul.

West Coast and in Canada. Vine Park opened in the fall, after state legislation made it legal for customers to handcraft small quantities of their own beer on site. Since then, the company has begun brewing small batches of beer for other local restaurants and has opened a brewpub and beer garden next door to the BOP site.

There were seven different brews on tap in the brewpub when we last visited; four of them can be brewed by a layperson in the brewery next door. Before choosing, a would-be brewer will want to sample these products:

- **Lazy Days Pale Ale** is a medium-bodied amber brew with a hoppy flavor.

- **Walnut Brown Ale** has a sweet and nutty taste with a light coffee undertone.

- **Eelpout Stout**, full-bodied and bittersweet, is an Irish-style stout.

- **Slapshot Hard Cider** offers both tang and sweetness.

A sampler of all the above, in 5-oz. glasses, is available. Other brews on tap include:

- **Northern Lights Ale**, a crisp, mild-flavored golden ale with a touch of wheat.

- **Celebration Lager** is made with German malt and yeast. Vine Parkers say one taste will transport you to Bavaria.

- **Justus Ramsey Red** is a full-bodied amber brew with a slightly sweet, smoky, caramel flavor.

- Any of a number of constantly changing guest brews.

How involved does the guest brewer have to get? He or she initially spends less than two hours choosing and adding ingredients to the brewing kettle. The second step, which takes two weeks, is performed by the experts and involves fermenting, aging, and filtering the batch. Finally, the guest returns for two hours to fill, cap, label, and sample his or her work. The yield is 12.5 gallons, which results in 72 22-oz. bottles of your very own beer. Amaze, as they say, your friends. Among several deals here, there is a frequent-brewer program.

A first-time brewer may work up an appetite; hence the pub and beer garden. Appetizers here are called shared plates and might be chorizo pizza, beer-flavored palm dip, or smoked oyster fritters. Soups and salads are available, including smoked duck chili, a Vine Park exclusive. Sandwiches include burgers, a mahi-mahi po' boy, and chicken salad. (A nice lunch selection is half a club sandwich, served with soup or salad.) Larger plates include stout-smoked duck and cider-cured pork chop. If there is room, the brown ale bread pudding and the chocolate cake are tempting.

Should you happen in during a spell of warm weather, visit the beer garden out back and inquire about the strange little limestone cottage found there. It once housed Justus Ramsey, a real-estate developer and brother of a famous Minnesota politician.

W. A. Frost & Company

374 Selby Avenue
St. Paul, MN 55102
Telephone: (651) 224-5715
Web site: http://wafrost.citysearch.com/
Hours: 11 a.m.-1 a.m. Monday-Saturday,
10:30 a.m.-11 p.m. Sunday. Closed major holidays.
Nearby attraction: The State Capitol.

The dining room, with its four fireplaces and lush décor, has rightly been called the most romantic dining spot in the Twin Cities. That isn't meant to slight the separate bar, with its tin ceiling and rich, dark wood. Both sides of W. A. Frost are worth a visit. Still, most people arrive for a meal, with reservations, looking freshly scrubbed and well dressed.

A traveler should give this establishment credit: while it has received awards for the quality and quantity of its wine vintages, it stocks an awesome number of beers and ales. On tap are Leinenkugel, Full Sail Amber Ale, Guinness Stout, Double Diamond, Michelob Golden Draft Light, and Black and Tan, a mix of Guinness and a lighter-colored ale. Among bottled beers, there are a dozen from U. S. microbreweries, eight from larger American breweries, and a staggering, so to speak, 30 or so imports.

A litmus test as to whether a place knows beer may be whether they offer any of the ambrosial products from the Kalamazoo Brewing Company, maker of Bell's. Here, amber and porter are stocked. So are four kinds of Summit, James Page Amber Ale, Schell Pils, and more. Exotic imports run the gamut, from Canada's Cross Cut Stout to Belgium's Red Cap. If you have a microbrewed or foreign favorite, either look at the long beer menu or take a chance and order it. Single-malt scotches, hot drinks, mixed drinks, and, of course, wines are also quite popular.

There are separate restaurant and bar menus. In the bar, appetizers such as homemade focaccia and antipasto look great. The appetizer for the guy or girl who wants to be alone has to be roasted whole garlic. We were here in the fall, which no doubt accounted for a salad of autumn field greens and a soup of roasted sugar pumpkin puree. Yes, burgers are available, along with other sandwiches, cheese trays, and desserts. Thoughtfully, for anyone driving, Frost has an assortment of gourmet coffee.

For those who intend to dine as well as drink, the lunch and dinner menus have an embarrassment of riches. Promising luncheon items include grilled salmon, mushroom risotto, or one of several pastas. At night, we like grilled venison, stewed monkfish served with shellfish and new potatoes, or an autumn cassoulet containing ham sausage and a duck leg. Several dishes, in-

W. A. Frost & Company, St. Paul.

cluding risotto, can be found on all menus. The patio offers warm-weather opportunities for dining and drinking

W. A. Frost is an example of the positive aspects of urban renewal. The Cathedral Hill district, which started out as a lavish place, deteriorated following World War II. This was an abandoned building that some people with vision returned to its former glory. They spent money: while the tin ceiling is original, décor such as the back bar was installed after being salvaged from a place in Superior, Wisconsin. So when you visit and admire the splendor, do not assume it all happened by accident.

The Wild Onion

788 Grand Avenue
St. Paul, MN 55105
Telephone: (651) 291-2525
Hours: 11 a.m.-1 a.m. (bar); 11 a.m.-11 p.m. (kitchen).
Nearby attraction: The scene along Grand Avenue.

The Wild Onion, St. Paul.

A mentally and physically healthful way to work off an extra brew or two is to cavort on the dance floor. Not many taverns in this book offer an opportunity to dance, so when one comes along it should be noted.

The Wild Onion, in business since May 1997, gives customers the services of a disc jockey six nights a week. The DJ sets up about 9 p.m. and before 10 he is spinning pop, rock, rockabilly, swing, jazz, country—just about anything but rap and hiphop. The tunes continue until 1 p.m. Monday-Saturday.

Music and a place to put down some steps are just two of the ideas Tom, the owner, came up with when he started the Wild Onion. Another is lots and lots of beer varieties. There are, for example, 21 national, local, microbrew, and imported tap handles awaiting your pleasure at the bar. They are backed by about the same number of bottles. There are little or no overlaps between tap and bottle, giving the prospective beer drinker a nice array of choices.

Happy hour runs 3-6 p.m. Monday-Friday and offers a dollar off on 20-oz. tappers, domestic bottled brews for $1.75, a mere $3 for a glass of house wine, $4 for a top-shelf martini, as well as a buffet of hors d'oeuvres. This is yet another place where a patio beckons whenever the weather permits.

"We have to have patio service to remain competitive," Tom says, appreciating the irony of a state like Minnesota offering many places to dine and drink outside. Inside, the menu offers some interesting lunch and dinner choices. A turkey melt sandwich with cranberry mayonnaise is popular, as are Cajun pork chops, reddened chicken, and a signature chop salad.

The food is several notches above typical bar fare and may of course be enjoyed at bar or table. The crowd includes a range of adults and families for lunch or dinner but grows younger as the DJ tunes up and the hour grows late. Except for folks who dress up for work and stop here for a meal or on the way home, the customers are casually attired.

Tom describes the Wild Onion as a Chicago-style tavern with an eclectic menu and a casual atmosphere. Whether you are dining, drinking, dancing, or all of the above, you're bound to enjoy yourself at one of Grand Avenue's more popular haunts.

HASTINGS

Hastings, population 18,034, boasts a whopping 63 buildings on the National Register of Historic Places. A look at the map tells why: the Mississippi, St. Croix, and Vermillion rivers all rendezvous here, making it a natural spot for Victorian settlers to stop and to stay.

The town, in the Hiawatha Valley, is blessed with a climate sufficiently benign to allow a local winery to use its own grapes in its vintages. Those who would rather shop than check on the harvest can visit the many antique stores, gift shops, and boutiques. Or they can glimpse the lazy rivers from one of several pleasant parks. Small wonder this town, less than 20 miles from downtown St. Paul, has been picked as one of Minnesota's "Best Day Trips" by a Twin Cities newspaper.

For additional information, contact the Hastings Area Chamber of Commerce and Tourism Bureau by dialing (888) 612-6122 or (651) 437-6775. Or, see www.hastingsmn.org

---

Bierstube

109 Eleventh Street West
Hastings, MN 55033
Telephone: (651) 437-8259
and
6434 Cahille Avenue
Inver Grove Heights, MN 55076
Telephone: (651) 451-8073
Hours: 11 a.m.-1 a.m. Monday-Saturday, 11 a.m.-11 p.m. Sunday (bar); 11 a.m.-midnight Monday-Saturday, 11 a.m.-11 p.m. Sunday (kitchen). Closed Thanksgiving, Christmas.
Nearby attraction: Afton State Park.

What we have here are two affiliated taverns, both named Bierstube, both on the southeast side of the metropolitan area, serving similar beverages and fare, in similar buildings.

There are differences, of course. The Hastings location is, in our mind, easier to find. It is a block west of Highway 61, which also serves as Main Street

Bierstube, Hastings.

through this picturesque town. You will know you've arrived if you look across the street and see the high school football stadium.

The Inver Grove Heights Bierstube deserves its own paragraph for directions. From downtown St. Paul, head south on Highway 52. Once you are in Inver Grove Heights, exit left or east onto Upper 55th Street. Upper 55th crests a hill and ends, where you should turn right and drive through two stoplights to this Bierstube. It will have been about nine blocks from where you last turned. It is in a small strip mall that also houses a pizzeria, a beauty parlor, and a church. Obviously, this location can meet a variety of needs.

Why stop at either place? The on-tap beer shows that the Bierstubes respect their customers. In Hastings, the handles produce Coors Light, Hacker-Pschorr, Hamm's, Paulaner Oktoberfest, Schell Dark, and Bierstube Red, the last made for the two 'stubes by Schell. In Inver Grove, a tapper might be Bierstube Red, Bud Light, Leinenkugel Honey Weiss, Miller Golden Draft, Paulaner Oktoberfest, or Schell Dark.

These are relaxing places in which to sip a brew, and they are popular locally. Suburbanites come here for burgers and for steaks, though each menu has a couple of authentic German dishes. When we last spoke with a Bierstube manager during the Christmas holidays, he had to stop the conversation momentarily so that he could sell a gift certificate to a patron.

The jukeboxes offer a little bit of everything, there are T-shirts for collectors of souvenirs, and as for happy hours, a manager said, "Happy hour? Every hour you spend here is happy!" The homeward-bound accountants, insurance brokers, and state budget analysts who stop for a brew before dinner would surely agree.

LAKELAND

There are 2,066 souls here, and many of their homes face Lake St. Croix, the widest portion of the St. Croix River that separates Minnesota from Wisconsin. Upriver about 12 miles from where the St. Croix meets the Mississippi, Lakeland appears to have been a resort community at one time, before some folks realized it was also a very short commute into St. Paul.

Those who have just entered Minnesota might also want to continue a couple of miles on I-94 so that they can stop at the St. Croix Travel Information Center. The center offers a bevy of vacation and weekend tips for every corner of the state.

The Bungalow Inn

1151 River Crest Road
Lakeland, MN 55043
Telephone: (651) 436-5005
Hours: 11 a.m.-1 a.m. (bar); 11 a.m.-9 p.m. Monday-Thursday, 11 a.m.-1 a.m. Friday, 8 a.m.-1 a.m. Saturday, 8 a.m.-9 p.m. Sunday (kitchen). Closed Thanksgiving, Christmas Eve, Christmas Day, New Year's Eve, New Year's Day.
Nearby attraction: The St. Croix River.

Consider this a vote in a couple of categories for the Bungalow Inn. This comfy tavern is the first place for a traveler to enjoy food and drink after leaving Wisconsin. The route is simple: Head west out of the Badger State on I-94, crossing the St. Croix River at what appears to be its broadest point. Turn right or north immediately on Highway 95 and look to the right. The modest, cream-colored exterior of the Bungalow should be in sight.

Our visit took place at noon on a Friday. We ordered the fish fry and were rewarded with a very tasty, deep-fried cod, slaw, and fries to go with our beer. A neat trick is performed at the bar. Diners are given a wooden tray that fits over the bar's curved wooden edge. This puts diners within easy reach of their food and prevents dribbling food from the plate to the mouth.

The folks we saw enjoying themselves at lunch seemed to like it here, perhaps realizing that friendly, unpretentious spots are all too few. There seemed to be a table of grandmas, a couple of electrical contractors, a table of women friends, a table of guys perhaps from the local phone company, and various savvy drivers fresh off the interstate. Soft music plays whenever the jukebox is silent. The box is an old Wurlitzer, which is quite picturesque while offering up-to-date tunes. Rock, country, ballads, movie themes, love songs—plug the player, which is filled with compact discs, and take your choice.

There are choices to be made at the beer tap, too. Someone with beer knowledge has ensured that customers can order Newcastle Ale, Paulaner, Leinenkugel Honey Weiss, Guinness, and at least two other imported tap beers. There are additional interesting brews, as well as beers anyone might expect, in bottle form. Wine and liquor are available.

Besides the fish fry all day Friday, check out a clubhouse sandwich or a New York Rueben for lunch. At dinner, consider the meals listed under Bungalow Originals: shrimp, walleye, or reddened chicken breasts (breasts pan fried with roasted red peppers). There also are appetizers, soups, salads, and entrees such as steaks and chops on the full menu. And don't forget breakfast on either weekend day.

What with the genial people and all that good beer on tap, it's only logical that the bar be large and offer plenty of seating. It is U-shaped, making any table easy to spot if you are awaiting one. A pair of TV sets cling to the rafters, but they aren't all that intrusive. For those who want to remember where in Minnesota they may have had their first cold draft, souvenir sweaters and jackets are available.

NORTH ST. PAUL

This is an unassuming place, a Twin Cities suburb filled with business and industry and sturdy housing. It's nicely located, just inside the Interstate 694 loop and served by busy east-west Highway 36. The latter stretch of road begins in Stillwater and ends at a point near where St. Paul and Minneapolis meet. With a population of 12,836, there could be no more fitting a locale for the state's oldest tavern than North St. Paul.

For additional information, contact the St. Paul Area Chamber of Commerce, (651) 223-5000.

Neumann's Bar and Grill

2531 Seventh Avenue
North St. Paul, MN 55109
Telephone: (651) 770-6020
Hours: 10 a.m.-1 a.m. (bar); 11 a.m.-10 p.m. (kitchen).
Nearby attraction: Year-round ice skating at the John Rose Oval Skating Center.

One hundred fifteen years and counting. That is how long Neumann's has been serving up food and drink from this location on the same Seventh Avenue that runs from here southwest, darn near to Minneapolis–St. Paul International Airport. In point of fact, Neumann's is the oldest continuously operating tavern in the state. So please—show a little respect.

This is an ideal tavern. The customers are everyday people, here for lunch, for a few brews, for the live music on weekends, or for all of the above. Besides a number of interesting bottles in the cooler, there are eight different beers on tap: Summit, Amstel Light, Hamm's, Leinenkugel Honey Weiss, Budweiser, Bud Light, Miller Golden Draft, and Miller Lite. Wine and liquor are available, too, but beer is the big drink here.

With those beers go any of a number of tasty sandwiches. Look for cod, steak, chicken, ham and cheese, turkey, a meatball hoagie, a Big Jim Burger or a Little Jim Burger (Jim once owned the place and his burgers still thrive). The best deal on sandwiches are the specials, available with chips. In warm weather, food and drink are served on a patio well shielded from any street noise.

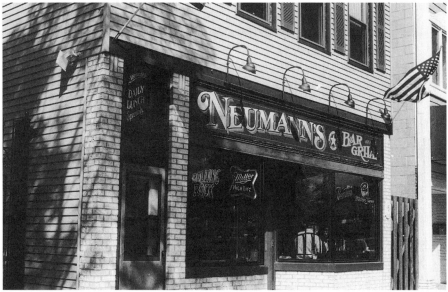

Neumann's Bar and Grill, North St. Paul.

Besides its reputation for longevity, Neumann's is known as a spot where quality musicians come to play, beginning at 8 p.m. on Fridays and Saturdays. The last time we stopped, folks such as Steve Vactor and Michelle Dukark; the Rough Cuts; the Slim Hippos; the Blues Kings; Cool Disposition; Jack Knife & the Sharps; Blues Farm; and Powers Project were slated to play. The music may be rock, blues, rockabilly, folk/rock, or something akin. These are local musicians and they are good enough to draw decent crowds. There is no cover charge.

When the bands are elsewhere, the bartenders tune in any of 120 TV channels on a cable service; there is no jukebox. Souvenirs come in the form of sweatshirts, T-shirts, and hats. The crowd swells at lunch, tapers off a bit on weekday afternoons, then grows again with the after-work crowd. During softball season, Wednesday and Thursday nights are aflood with players, spouses, you name it. On weekends, Neumann's is a lively place until last call.

Because not all customers may be aware of Neumann's heritage, the menu relates a whimsical history of the place. It notes that the tavern stayed open during Prohibition by selling near-beer over the bar and homemade booze upstairs! There was a bait store in the basement, where a fisher could pick up minnows, worms, and popskull of one sort or another.

The back bar, a handsome achievement in wood and glass, was installed by the Hamm's brewery. Hamm's has been on tap here for approximately 76 years. For a number of years there was a picture of Charles Atlas, clad only in a fig leaf, on the wall of the women's restroom. If a woman lifted the fig leaf, a buzzer went off that could be heard throughout the old tavern. All that ended when an irate woman, leaf in hand, ripped Charlie off the wall.

STILLWATER

If there is a tourism alternative to going up north and getting a cabin on the lake, this is it. Stillwater, population 16,193, offers a chance to go for a sail and, after shopping and a good meal, head to a bed-and-breakfast for the evening. Yes, this is an unapologetically artsy, shop-till-you-drop sort of destination.

On the west bank of the St. Croix River and across the water from Wisconsin, the town is a historic place, proud of its early lumberjack days, when the St. Croix thickened each spring with logs. Nowadays, sleek sailboats and swift cruisers ply the waters; many Twin Cities residents keep their watercraft here. It also is the home of the Zephyr, a vintage dining train, and nearly three dozen golf courses.

Highway 36 connects Stillwater with St. Paul and Minneapolis, about 45 minutes away. To find out more, contact the Greater Stillwater Chamber of Commerce at (651) 439-4001, or go to the Internet and look for www.ilovestillwater.com.

Freight House

305 Water Street South
Stillwater, MN 55082
Telephone: (651) 439-5718
Hours: 11 a.m.-8 p.m. Sunday-Thursday, 11 a.m.-9 p.m. Friday-Saturday (restaurant); 8 p.m.-1 a.m. Friday-Saturday (night club). Closed New Year's Day.
Nearby attraction: St. Croix River.

Formerly a Burlington Northern train station, the Freight House is on the National Register of Historic Places. Character oozes from the cozy bars, the old-time Stillwater photos displayed on the wall, and the carousel horses hanging from the restaurant's high-beamed ceiling.

About the only reason not to go to the Freight House would be if you were trying to dodge Twin Cities residents. That is because folks who live in Minneapolis and St. Paul make the pilgrimage to Stillwater generally, and the Freight House specifically, in droves.

And why not? Besides being large and accommodating, the destination offers a good place to eat and a nightclub with either a deejay or a band. Did we mention that there are five bars spread over the approximately 30,000 square feet? There are.

The five include a bar within the restaurant, two in the nightclub, and two on "the best deck in Minnesota," according to an employee. Draft spigots pour forth Leinenkugel Honey Weiss, Summit, Budweiser, Michelob Golden Light, Miller Golden Draft, and Miller Lite. Numerous other beers can be had by the bottle.

The restaurant serves beer-friendly food such as pastas, salads, burgers, other sandwiches, and steaks. There is a children's menu if you are traveling with the kids. Speaking of consumption, the place is packed on weekends with those who come for eats and drinks and stay for the tunes.

Perhaps the most unusual method of arrival is nautical. The big brick-and-wood structure is a mere 50 feet from the St. Croix River. It is not much of a hardship to point your sea legs toward dry land in this chichi old town.

Telephone ahead to find out who might be playing, or for directions in case you forget these: From the Twin Cities, head east on Hwy. 36 to Stillwater. At Hwy. 95, turn left and drive to the first light. Take a right there, which is Nelson Street, and look for the Freight House ahead on the left.

Especially in the summer, the Freight House can be overrun—the immediate Stillwater area is a top spot to recreate. Better to either get here early or pay a weekday visit. Bicyclists, kayakers, canoeists, wind- and fuel-powered sailors, hikers, rock climbers, shoppers, layabouts, idlers, families, and retirees all seem to stop in.

Have a brew, dine, and come away with a shirt, a cap, or related souvenir.

Gasthaus Bavarian Hunter

8390 Lofton Ave.
Stillwater, MN 55082
Telephone: (651) 439-7128
Web site: www.gasthausbavarianhunter.com
Hours: 11 a.m.-until all are gone (bar); 11 a.m.-9 p.m.
Mon.-Thurs.; 11 a.m.-10 p.m. Fri.; noon-10 p.m. Sat.;
noon-8 p.m. Sun. Closed major holidays.
Nearby attraction: The St. Croix River.

At the Gasthaus, just west of Stillwater, drinkers and diners are treated to a cozy, warm, authentic Bavarian atmosphere. Co-owners and husband and wife Carl and Kim are the real thing. Both of his parents and one of hers were German citizens. The culinary results are rewarding.

But like many rewards, this one takes a bit of exertion. The Gasthaus was built down a dead-end road, so travelers need to turn north off Highway 36 at the garden center just west of the shopping center, then drive for 2.5 miles. Once they cross the railroad tracks, an immediate left turn is in order. One more immediate left and the attractive, Bavarian lodge-style building and grounds will come into view on the right. About the only things missing are the mountains of Bavaria.

Gasthaus Bavarian Hunter, Stillwater.

TAVERNS WHERE YOU'RE
most likely to see . . .

- **A Back-door Political Deal:** Costello's, St. Paul.

- **Your Son or Daughter:** Stub & Herb's, followed closely by the Borealis, both of which are in Dinkytown, near the University of Minnesota.

- **The Guy who Caught the Big Fish:** Main Street Bar and Grill, Warroad.

- **Hockey Moms and Dads:** American Legion Post 24, Roseau.

- **Guys and Gals in Snowmobile Attire:** Black Cat Sports Bar & Grill, Thief River Falls.

- **The Next Big Hollywood Star:** Bryant-Lake Bowl, Minneapolis.

- **The Most Earnest Conversation:** Lucia's, Minneapolis.

- **The Least Earnest Conversation:** Lee's Liquor Lounge, Minneapolis.

- **Writers and Poets:** Kieran's, Minneapolis.

- **A Man or Woman Whose Parents Spoke German:** Turner Hall, New Ulm.

- **A Man or Woman Whose Parents Rode Harleys:** Jonny's Saloon, Elba.

- **The Best Musicians:** Lee's Liquor Lounge, Minneapolis, with a nod to Neumann's Bar and Grill in North St. Paul.

- **The Best Dancers:** The Wild Onion, St. Paul.

Immediately inside, on the right, is the bar. Ten German imports are on tap here, primarily Hacker-Pschorr, Paulaner, or Spaten light, dark, or weiss beers. Four more German brews are available in bottles. If a meal is to follow time spent on a barstool, ask the bartender for a menu and decide what to order. Then he or she will let you know which of the gourmet beers goes best with your food. Wine and liquor are available, and the German white wines are especially popular. So are German brandies and shots of schnapps and other potent beverages.

Kim says the crowd is primarily local and regional, people who either have a hankering for real German food or are exercising their heritage. In terms of miscellaneous information about all things German, the bar is a rich place to strike up a conversation. In the summer, an occasional European tourist can be found hoisting a brew. The most popular meals tend to be jager schnitzel (breaded pork cutlets with a savory mushroom sauce) and sauerbraten, which is thinly sliced and marinated roast beef.

Friday evenings and Sunday afternoons feature a strolling accordion player. The music is as faithfully reproduced as the décor, which features dark wood but is anything but depressing. Besides T-shirts, sweatshirts, and glassware, those traditional, hefty beer mugs are available as souvenirs. Summer evenings are long, so if weather permits, ask to be seated on the deck. Gasthaus has been serving German beer and food since 1966. At the bar or at a table, this is a bustling and friendly place.

Meister's
901 South Fourth St.
Stillwater, MN 55082
Telephone: (651) 439-9860
Hours: 11 a.m.-1 a.m. (bar); 11 a.m.-12:30 a.m. (grill).
Closed major holidays.
Nearby attraction: The lift bridge on the St. Croix River.

Stillwater, as we have noted, is a tourist town. All year round, the visitors pull into town, clogging the main street (Highway 95) and doing things like shopping, dining, gawking, and relaxing. That's fine, but for the fact that the locals sometimes need a place to get away. Meister's is that place.

Since 1948, the stucco tavern at the corner of Osgood (Fourth) and Churchill streets has been a retreat for those in the know. The place is a mile north of Highway 36, the multilane road that runs between here and the Twin Cities. While Stillwater's most famous residents, Jessica Lang and husband Sam Shepherd, might not frequent the place, a visitor can find some St. Paul people who are stars in their own right.

Those folks come for a cold beer, among other attractions. Tappers include Budweiser, Leinenkugel, Michelob Golden Light, Miller Genuine Draft, Paulaner Oktoberfest, Paulaner Hefe Weizen, and Schmidt. Bottled beer is available and includes a large number of imports. Wine and mixed drinks also stand ready.

Locals also make the scene to avail themselves of the menu, which is bar food and more. The most popular sandwich for lunch is the Meisterburger, a one-third pound of ground beef cooked with real bacon bits and cheese. A rarity on the sandwich list that attracted our eye was the Coney Island. Call them Coneys, Sloppy Joes, or whatever, the taste of ground beef in a flavorful, tomato-based sauce is one we never tire of. It works well with beer.

Other foods include bratwurst or Polish sausage sandwiches. Dinner favorites include home-smoked ribs, T-bone steak, and deep-fried shrimp. For insurance purposes, says Tom Meister, one of the owners, there is no happy hour. Rather, Meister's features regularly scheduled "beer specials." They also make available hats, T-shirts, and sweatshirts. The place is one huge room and has something of a Germanic look and feel to it.

Meister's is, says Tom, "the steadiest bar business in the area." That may be because it has been in family hands for two generations. The tavern was opened by Tom's late father and is currently run by Tom and brother Steve. Their mom, Eileen, comes in occasionally and is well known to regular customers. In a high-traffic, retailing town like Stillwater, this is a rock of permanence a few blocks from places that may be here today and gone tomorrow.

APPENDIX A

Minnesota "Beer Weather" Festivals and Events

(We won't guarantee great beer at every gathering listed below. But we do pledge that there are fun people at these mostly outdoor festivals and events, creating a nice atmosphere.)

MAY

Festival of Nations, St. Paul.
Cinco de Mayo Fiesta, St. Paul.
Flower Power, Minneapolis.

JUNE

Buffalo Days, Luverne.
Dam Days, Morristown.
Friendly City Days, Albertville.
Arts and River Festival, Winona.
Land of the Loon Arts and Crafts Festival, Virginia.
Rochesterfest, Rochester.
Heritage Festival, Faribault.
International Polkafest, Chisholm.
Scandinavian Hjemkomst Festival, Moorhead.
Minnesota Street Rod Association's Back to the 50s, St. Paul.
Park Point Art Fair, Duluth.
Gay-Lesbian-Bisexual-Transgender Pride Festival, Minneapolis.
Tater Daze, Brooklyn Park.

JULY

Funfest, Eagan.
Spam Town USA Festival, Austin.
Rodeo and Bull Ridin' Bonanza, Hamel.
Heritage Days Celebration, Two Harbors.
Showboat Days, Minneapolis.
Moondance Jam, Walker.

Heritagefest, New Ulm.
First City Celebration of Music and the Arts, Bemidji.
Aquatennial, Minneapolis.
Riverfest and Art Fair, Anoka.
Phelps Mill Festival, Underwood.
Hoedown, Houston.
Kolacky Days, Montgomery.

AUGUST

Derby Days, Shakopee.
Giant Celebration, LeSeuer.
Loring Park Art Festival, Minneapolis.
Uptown Art Fair, Minneapolis.
International Folk Festival, Duluth.
Tall Timber Days Festival, Grand Rapids.
All Slav Days and Grape Festival, Chisholm.
Irish Fair, St. Paul.
Minnesota Renaissance Festival, Shakopee.
Potato Days Festival, Barnesville.
Stiftungfest, Norwood-Young America.
Woodbury Days,Woodbury.

SEPTEMBER

Defeat of Jessie James Days, Northfield.
Rheinfest on the Mississippi, St. Paul.
Arts and Crafts Fair, Little Falls.
Rock Bend Folk Festival, St. Peter.
Czech and Slovak Day, St. Paul.
Dozinky, New Prague.
Air Fest and Balloon Rally, Faribault.
Grape Stomp and Fall Festival, Alexandria.
Tree Frog Music Festival, Faribault.
Pumpkin Patch Festival, Litchfield.

OCTOBER

Oktoberfest, New Ulm.
Celebrazione Italiana, Little Canada.
Fall Festival of the Arts, Red Wing.

APPENDIX B

Sorting out Minnesota's Liquor Laws

The Department of Public Safety controls the sale of liquor—and gambling, for that matter—in the state of Minnesota. An expert in the department's St. Paul office recently admitted that the laws and rules governing alcoholic beverages are complex. Nevertheless, here are some facts for the tavern visitor.

First and most important, the law regarding driving while intoxicated (DWI) states that .10 is the point at which a driver is impaired and may be charged. That is more than two 12-oz. beers consumed per hour for an adult male of average size and weight. Smaller males and females will violate the DWI statute if they attempt to keep up with that full-sized adult.

No 3.2 percent beer is sold over the bar, but lots of it is sold as packaged goods, or "off" sales. What determines, when buying a six pack, whether it will contain more or less than 3.2 percent alcohol? Content hinges on what kind of license the retailer possesses. What determines the kind of license? Cities and counties set the kind and number. Incidentally, the number of "on" sales places (taverns permitted to sell alcohol by the drink) is determined strictly by population. Consequently, any municipality has the same number of bars per capita as, say, Minneapolis or St. Paul.

Or do they? With an eye toward local control, the legislature some time ago decided that the rules of cities and counties could be more restrictive than those of the state, if they so chose. They are not permitted to be less restrictive. The Department of Public Safety also reports that, much to the relief of beer drinkers, there are no dry cities or towns.

Now that you know a few rules, here is when you can apply them. On-premises sales can take place any time after 8 a.m. and prior to 1 a.m., seven days a week. Off-premises sales can occur any time after 8 a.m. or before 8 p.m. or 10 p.m., depending on day of the week and size of the city. First-class cities (the large ones) may sell packaged goods until 8 p.m. Monday-Thursday and until 10 p.m. Friday-Saturday. All other municipalities can sell packaged goods until 10 p.m. There are no legal package-goods sales on Sunday.

INDEX

More Great Titles

FROM TRAILS BOOKS & PRAIRIE OAK PRESS

ACTIVITY GUIDES

Great Minnesota Walks: 49 Strolls, Rambles, Hikes,
and Treks, *Wm. Chad McGrath*

Great Wisconsin Walks: 45 Strolls, Rambles,
Hikes, and Treks, *Wm. Chad McGrath*

Acorn Guide to Northwest Wisconsin, *Tim Bewer*

Paddling Illinois: 64 Great Trips by Canoe and Kayak. *Mike Svob*

Paddling Southern Wisconsin: 82 Great Trips by Canoe and Kayak, *Mike Svob*

Paddling Northern Wisconsin: 82 Great Trips by Canoe and Kayak, *Mike Svob*

Wisconsin Underground: A Guide to Caves, Mines, and
Tunnels in and around the Badger State, *Doris Green*

TRAVEL GUIDES

Great Little Museums of the Midwest, *Christine des Garennes*

Great Minnesota Weekend Adventures, *Beth Gauper*

The Great Wisconsin Touring Book: 30 Spectacular Auto Tours, *Gary Knowles*

Tastes of Minnesota: A Food Lover's Tour, *Donna Tabbert Long*

Wisconsin Lighthouses: A Photographic
and Historical Guide, *Ken and Barb Wardius*

Wisconsin Waterfalls, *Patrick Lisi*

Wisconsin Family Weekends: 20 Fun Trips for
You and the Kids, *Susan Lampert Smith*

County Parks of Wisconsin, Revised Edition, *Jeannette and Chet Bell*

Up North Wisconsin: A Region for All Seasons, *Sharyn Alden*

The Spirit of Door County: A Photographic Essay, *Darryl R. Beers*

Great Wisconsin Taverns: 101 Distinctive Badger Bars, *Dennis Boyer*

Great Weekend Adventures, *the Editors of Wisconsin Trails*

The Wisconsin Traveler's Companion: A Guide to
Country Sights, *Jerry Apps and Julie Sutter-Blair*

NATURE ESSAYS
Wild Wisconsin Notebook, *James Buchholz*
Trout Friends, *Bill Stokes*
Northern Passages: Reflections from Lake Superior Country, *Michael Van Stappen*
River Stories: Growing up on the Wisconsin, *Delores Chamberlain*

HOME & GARDEN
Creating a Perennial Garden in the Midwest, *Joan Severa*
Wisconsin Garden Guide, *Jerry Minnich*
Wisconsin Herb Cookbook, *Suzanne Breckenridge & Marjorie Snyder*
Bountiful Wisconsin: 110 Favorite Recipes, *Terese Allen*
Hometown Flavor: A Cook's Tour, *Terese Allen*

HISTORICAL BOOKS
Prairie Whistles: Tales of Midwest Railroading, *Dennis Boyer*
Barns of Wisconsin, *Jerry Apps*
Portrait of the Past: A Photographic Journey Through Wisconsin 1865-1920, *Howard Mead, Jill Dean, and Susan Smith*
Wisconsin: The Story of the Badger State, *Norman K. Risjord*

GHOST STORIES
Haunted Wisconsin, *Michael Norman and Beth Scott*
W-Files: True Reports of Wisconsin's Unexplained Phenomena, *Jay Rath*
Northern Frights: A Supernatural Ecology of the Wisconsin Headwaters, *Dennis Boyer*
Giants in the Land: Folktales and Legends of Wisconsin, *Dennis Boyer*

For a free catalog, phone, write, or e-mail us.

TRAILS BOOKS
P.O. Box 317, Black Earth, WI 53515
(800) 236-8088 • e-mail: books@wistrails.com
www.trailsbooks.com